The Real Story of the Whaler

The Real Story of the Whaler

Whaling, Past and Present

By A. Hyatt Verill

Copyright

Contents

Introduction

There is always a fascination about the lives of men who follow the sea and of all those who "go down to the sea in ships" the bravest, most adventurous and hardiest were the Yankee whalemen.

Many stories of whalers and whaling have been written, but in nearly every case a glamour of romance and mystery has been woven about the whalemen of fiction and a false idea has been created as to their lives, their calling and their voyages. But no fiction has ever been written which does justice to the indomitable courage, the reckless daring, the terrific dangers, the unspeakable hardships, the heart-breaking labor, the terrible privations, the inhuman brutality, and the sublime heroism which were all in the day's work of the whalemen. To the Yankee whalers our country owes a debt of gratitude which can never be repaid, and no man is more worthy of a niche in America's Hall of Fame or a prominent place in our history than the weather-beaten, old-time whaler of New England.

For more than two centuries they scoured the seven seas and built the prosperity and progress of New England by pitting their lives against those of the mighty monsters of the deep. But the very wealth, progress and civilization which they helped to establish resulted in their downfall, until today the Yankee whaler is a figure of the past. This book has been written to give a true and unvarnished idea of the whalemen's lives, their adventures and hardships, the means by which their quarry was sought and captured, their vessels and their voyages. It is intended not as a history of the whaling industry nor as a technical description of whaling methods but rather as a narrative of a whaleman's life embodying details of the chase, the vessels and their equipment, the whales and their habits, the dangers incident to whaling, the labors and privations of everyday occurrence, the voyages made and true stories of the sea.

Volumes might be written on the subject and much would still be left unrecorded, for whaling was a profession built up by many generations and by actual experience and the mass of technical details connected with the occupation is overwhelming. Only the more important, interesting or salient features and incidents have been included in this work and if it leads to a better and more sympathetic knowledge of the whalers, a realization of what we owe them, a truer insight into their lives, and at the same time interests the reader the author's aim will be accomplished.

To my many friends in New Bedford I wish to express my gratitude for innumerable courtesies and much invaluable aid without which the work of writing this book would have been a difficult task indeed. Particularly am I indebted to Mr. Frank Wood and to Mr. Pemberton H. Nye; to the former for permitting free access to the priceless records and wonderful collections of the Old Dartmouth Historical Society and to the latter for advice, information and suggestions such as could only have been obtained from one who has actually taken part in the scenes described.

FEW OF US REALIZE how much we owe the whalers, the prominent part they played in our history, the prosperity and wealth they brought to the infant Republic, or the influence their rough and ready lives had upon the civilization, exploration and commerce of the globe.

The first time the Stars and Stripes were unfurled in a British port they snapped in the wind of the English Channel at a whaler's masthead. The first time Old Glory was seen on the western coast of South America it soared aloft to a whaleship's truck, and far and wide, to the desolate Arctic, to the palm-fringed islands of the tropics, to the coral shores of the South Seas – to every land washed by the waves of any ocean – the banner of our land was carried by the Yankee whaling skippers.

No sea was too broad for the whalers to cross; no land too remote, too wild or too forbidding for them to visit. The crushing icefloes of the Arctic, the vast desolation of the Antarctic, the uncharted reefs of the Pacific or the cannibals[1] of Polynesia held no terrors for the weather-beaten whalemen of New Bedford or Nantucket. In many a new-found land, on many an unknown island, the naked savages saw white men for the first time when a bluff-bowed, dingy-sailed whaleship dropped anchor off their shores. Nearly half a century before Paul Revere made his famous ride the hardy whalemen of Massachusetts had sought their quarry in the waters north of Davis Straits. It was a Nantucket whaleman, Captain Folger, who first sketched the Gulf Stream and its course, and this rude drawing, engraved for Benjamin Franklin, revolutionized the commerce between Europe and America. Ten years before the first shot of the Revolution was fired whalemen pushed

---

[1] Herman Melville makes a reference to cannibalism being practiced in Nuku Hiva, French Polynesia in *Typee* (1846).

through the Arctic Ocean and sought the Northwest passage and within twelve years after the Declaration of Independence the whaling ship *Penelope* of Nantucket had cruised in waters farther north than were reached by any vessel for a century later.

By 1848 the bark *Superior* of Gay Head had penetrated Behring Straits and three years later the *Saratoga* of New Bedford reached 71° 40' north, fifteen miles nearer the pole than had been attained by the exploring ship *Blossom.* It was the reports of whalers that led Wilkes[2] on his famous explorations and years before Perry[3] opened the doors of Japan to commerce whalers had visited its shores, had cruised in its waters and one whaleman had lived among the Japanese and had taught them English.

Ever the first to penetrate unknown seas and to visit new lands, the whalers were the pioneers of exploration and blazed a trail for commerce, civilization and Christianity to follow. Knowing no fear, laughing at danger, self-reliant and accustomed to fighting against overwhelming odds, the whalemen performed many a deed of heroism and bravery of which the world never hears. It was the crews of the whaling ships *Magnolia* and *Edward* of New Bedford that saved the garrison of San Jose, California, from annihilation in 1846.[4] When the government buildings burned at Honolulu it was whalemen who saved the town, and when wars broke out and their country needed fighting men, the whalers were among the first to respond to the call to arms and much of our success in naval battles of the past was due to the men who had learned seamanship, courage and reckless daring in the hard school of whaling.

And how would it have fared with the American colonies if it had not been for the whalemen? Hardly had the

---

[2] American naval officer and explorer Charles Wilkes (1798-1877).
[3] Most likely a reference to Robert Peary (1856-1920), the famous Arctic explorer.
[4] During the Mexican American War of 1846 to 1848.

Pilgrims landed on Massachusetts' shores when the whale fishery was born and Cape Cod was settled mainly because of the abundance of whales in its waters. By 1639 the whales had become one of Massachusetts' greatest sources of revenue, and within the next two years Long Island was settled by whalers. So important did the colonists find this industry that in 1644 the town of Southampton was divided into four wards of eleven people each whose duty was to secure and cut up the whales that came ashore. At that time no ships had set forth in quest of whales and the whalemen depended upon those which could be captured from small boats and it was not until 1688 that the first whaleship set forth on a true whaling cruise.

In August of that year the Brigantine *Happy Return*, Timotheus Vanderuen, master, sailed out of Boston harbor bound for the Bahamas and Florida in search of sperm whales; the first of the fleet which later dotted the broad oceans of the world and made the name of New England famous in every land.

Within a dozen years the sails of sloops, brigs and schooners from Nantucket and other Massachusetts towns were spread to the winds of the Atlantic from the Arctic circle to the equator. Laden deep with oil the ships returned, and into the coffers of the little New England towns flowed a steady stream of gold.[5] Many of these coast towns, almost unknown to the people of the neighboring states, became famous throughout the world, and in many a distant land and to many a strange people the name of New Bedford, New London, Gay Head, Nantucket, Bristol or Sag Harbor was more familiar than New York, Washington or Boston. Upon the whalers such ports depended for their very existence, and to their hardy whaling sons

---

[5] American whale oil lit lamps across the world. In addition to providing illumination, byproducts of the whale were numerous, and included ambergris, candles, corset frames, fishing line, roofing material, and of course sustenance. The Inuit have long relied on the whale for their way of life, much as the Native Americans lived off the buffalo.

they owe the foundation of their present prosperity and standing. New Bedford in particular was built up by the whaling industry, and the skill, hardihood and daring of its whalemen brought fame and fortune to the town and made its name known in every seaport of the globe as the greatest of all whaling ports.

Although New Bedford no longer depends upon the whaling industry and has become a busy manufacturing town, much of the old atmosphere, many of the old land-marks and a great deal of interest still remain. The one-time whalers' boarding-houses and dancehalls, belonging to the Hetty Green property, still stand much as in days gone by and near them are the old storehouses where for-merly vast quantities – veritable fortunes – of whalebone were kept. The famous seamen's Bethel and sailors' home stands high above the neighboring buildings upon a little knoll, and in the Bethel one may read many cenotaphs erected to the memory of whalemen who met death during their long and dangerous cruises. Some of these are very quaint, and in stilted, old-fashioned phraseology relate thrilling tragedies of the sea in a few terse sentences as, for example, the following, which are two of the most note-worthy:

ERECTED BY THE OFFICERS AND CREW OF THE BARK *A. R. TUCKER* OF NEW BEDFORD TO THE MEMORY OF CHAS. H. PETTY OF WESTPORT, MASS. WHO DIED DEC. 14TH, 1863 IN THE 18TH YR. OF HIS AGE.

HIS DEATH OCCURRED IN 9 HRS. AFTER BEING BIT-TEN BY A SHARK WHILE BATHING NEAR THE SHIP HE WAS BURIED BY HIS SHIPMATES ON THE ISLAND OF DE LOSS,[6] NEAR THE COAST OF AFRICA.

---

[6] The Îles de Los are an island group lying off Conakry in Guinea, on the west coast of Africa.

IN MEMORY OF CAPT. WM. SWAIN ASSOCIATE MASTER OF THE CHRISTOPHER MITCHELL OF NANTUCKET. THIS WORTHY MAN AFTER FASTENING TO A WHALE WAS CARRIED OVERBOARD BY THE LINE AND DROWNED MAY 19TH, 1844 IN THE 49TH YR. OF HIS AGE.

BE YE ALSO READY, FOR IN SUCH AN HOUR AS YE THINK NOT THE SON OF MAN COMETH.

Many another tablet records a sudden death by violence, and yet not one whalemen in a thousand who found a grave in the vast depths of the oceans had friends or relatives to place a tablet to his memory in the little Bethel[7] of his home port. Only captains and officers were so honored, the common whaleman, the men who toiled and slaved and endured, were not worth recording; a bit of old sail was their winding sheet and coffin, the deep sea was their grave, and a line in a logbook their only epitaph. They died as they lived; unknown and unsung, mere units in the vast army of whalemen whose duty was to obey, who faced death unflinchingly and with a laugh or a curse; rough, vicious, brutal perhaps, but as brave as any men who ever trod a ship's deck.

From the windows of the Bethel and the home the seamen could look down upon the busy wharves along the waterfront and across the harbor to Fairhaven, on the farther shore, with a forest of masts and spars outlined against the water and the sky. Today the museum of the Old Dartmouth Historical Society obstructs the view and the forest of masts has disappeared. Along the docks a few schooners and perchance a brig or bark may lie moored; a few great casks of oil may be piled upon the wharves, and across the harbor a few famous old ships may be seen,

---

[7] Bethel Baptist church.

forsaken, dismantled and weather-beaten where they lie in the slips at the foot of shady streets and lanes.

Many a relic of the bygone days, when whaling was at its zenith, may still be seen in Fairhaven – such as the old candle factories, the blacksmith shops where lances, harpoons and other fittings were made and the boat yards where the whaleboats were built and the ships repaired.

It is in New Bedford itself, however, that one may obtain a true insight as to the whalers and their calling and in the building of the Historical Society on Water Street is the most complete whaling museum in all the world.[8] Here are hundreds of beautifully wrought ornaments, implements and utensils carved from whales' teeth and walrus' tusks by the whalemen during spare moments. Scores of whales' teeth engraved or *scrimshawed* by the whalers are also shown; there are models of whaling vessels made by the men themselves; letters written by them; paintings and drawings of famous vessels; priceless log-books and journals of the whalers as well as all the forms of lances, spades, guns and harpoons used in whaling; house-flags and figure-heads of famous ships, and tools and machines used in cutting blubber and trying out oil. A real whaleboat, which has seen active service, complete with all its equipment, occupies a prominent place in one room and best of all is a half-size model of a whaling ship, built to absolute scale and perfect in its every detail.

---

[8] Located in the colonial region of Old Dartmouth, Massachusetts.

2 - WHALES AND THEIR WAYS

IN ORDER TO OBTAIN an intelligent idea of whaling, to appreciate the perils and hardships of the calling and to understand the story of the whaler it is necessary to know something of the various kinds of whales and their habits, for there were many forms of whaling and the methods employed, the implements and weapons used and the dangers faced, depended upon the species of whale hunted.

A great many people think of whales as fish but in reality they are no more fish than are horses and cows.[9] Whales and all their relatives, such as porpoises, grampuses, and narwhals, are mammals – warm-blooded creatures which bring forth their young alive and suckle their offspring like any four-footed land mammal.

They also possess lungs and breathe air and are compelled to rise to the surface of the sea to breathe or "blow," and it is the air, warmed from their lungs and expelled as they take a fresh breath, which forms the little puff of vapor that often betrays a whale's presence. We often hear of whales "spouting" but in a strict sense they do not spout nor discharge water from their nose, although when wounded in a vital spot their breath is mixed with blood and they are said to "spout blood." Unlike whales, true fish are cold-blooded and lay eggs and instead of having lungs they are provided with gills which enable them to separate the oxygen from the water without coming to the surface. The confusion of whales with fish arises through the fact that whales are fish-like in form, are legless and hairless and live in the sea; but manatees and dugongs are hairless and have no true legs, and many seals also lack legs and

---

[9] Despite this fact, "fish" was the name bestowed upon whales by whalers.

live most of the time in the water and yet no one would dream of calling a seal a fish.

As a matter of fact the so-called "fins" or flippers of whales are really front legs which have been transformed to swimming organs, and if a whale's skeleton is examined we will find small bones which represent the hind legs of the whale's remote ancestors. Whalemen often speak of "taking a fish" of so many barrels and we frequently hear the term "whale fishery," but so we hear also of the "seal fishery," the "clam fishery," etc., and when a whaleman speaks of a "fish" he merely uses the vernacular and does not use the term through ignorance, for every whaleman knows full well that whales are mammals and not fishes.

There are a great many varieties of whales recognized by naturalists, but to the whalemen there were only six kinds of real whales.

These were the sperm whale, the right whale, the bow-head, the humpback, the sulphur-bottom and the finback.

In addition to these, there were the various porpoises, the grampus or blackfish, the narwhal or unicorn whale and the beluga or white whale, all of which were at times captured.

Each variety of the true whales has haunts and habits of its own and each furnishes oil and other products of distinct kinds and different values.

Of all the true whales the sperm whales and right whales were the most valuable and were the ones most widely sought. The right whales and bowheads are inhabitants of arctic and Antarctic waters and while the two are distinct, their habits, products, and the methods of hunting them are so similar that both may be considered together, the main difference being that the true right whales were hunted in the northern Pacific, Behring Sea and neighboring waters, whereas bowheads were denizens of the Arctic Ocean and Hudson Bay, while the Antarctic right whale was found in the waters of the Antarctic seas.[10]

The right whales and bowheads furnish oil and whalebone, the latter article formerly being among the most valuable of whale products, while the oil is not nearly as valuable as that obtained from the sperm whale.

The so-called "bone" of the right whale is in reality a hornlike material growing from the upper jaw of the whale in the form of a thick, flexible fringe. The lower jaw is very large and is shaped like an immense ladle or spoon and has no teeth. To the right whales and bowheads the whalebone or "baleen" serves as a strainer and is essential to the peculiar methods of feeding of these whales.

Opening his mouth, the right whale swims through the water until his great trough-like lower jaws is filled with small fish and marine animals. Then, closing his mouth the whale forces out the seawater through the fringe of whalebone, thus leaving the shrimps and other creatures it contained within his mouth, where they are confined by the gigantic strainer of baleen.

Owing to the enormous size of his jaws and the position of his eyes the right whale cannot see ahead of him, and owing to his habits, it is not necessary that he should, for his prey consists wholly of minute creatures, many of which are almost microscopic in size, and he trusts to luck in gathering everything within reach as he swims along like a mammoth scoop-net. As he has no teeth and as his jaws are useless as weapons of defense, nature has given him a wonderfully powerful and agile tail, and the right whale can sweep his tail, or "flukes," as the whalers call it, from eye to eye in a great half-circle and woe to any boat or enemy that comes within reach of this ponderous, thrashing mass of bone, flesh and sinew. The sperm

---

[10] The Biscay whale, small species of right whale, is a native of temperate and subtropical seas. This is the whale formerly abundant on the New England coast and which the early whalers of New England hunted. It is rare today, although specimens occasionally are captured on the southern shore of Long Island.

whales, of which there are several varieties, are all inhabitants of the broad oceans of temperate and tropical latitudes and are very different in habits, structure and appearance from the right whales and bowheads of the cold seas. The upper jaw of the sperm whale has no whalebone and no teeth, but the lower jaw, which is slender and sharp, bears a row of pointed, conical, white teeth as hard as ivory and these are as necessary to the sperm whale as the baleen to the right whale and bowheads.

Whereas the right whales swim along at or near the surface and scoop up tiny marine animals for their food, the sperm whales seek their food at the bottom of the sea and dive to great depths to secure the strange and powerful animals which form their diet. These are the giant cuttlefish or squids and many a battle royal must take place between the sperm whales and their enormous victims which lurk upon the floor of the ocean. With their sharp teeth and active jaws the whales seize the great squids,[11] tear them from their hold upon the rocks or bottom and bite them into bits, for the sperm whale's throat is very small – scarcely large enough to admit a man's fist – and only small morsels can be swallowed at a time. Of course, a great many of the squids secured by the whales are very small and offer but feeble resistance to their mammoth enemies, but others are of titanic size and must give the whales a hard tussle indeed.

No doubt the whales at times fall victims to their own prey, for the squids grow to a length of forty or fifty feet with ten long, flexible, snake-like tentacles armed with hundreds of great suckers. Moreover the squids possess enormous strength and are very tenacious of life and if such a monster once secured a good hold upon a whale he might well resist every effort of the latter long enough to drown the whale.

---

[11] The largest giant squid ever captured (on record) was just shy of 43 feet long.

That such tragedies of the deep actually occur is beyond question, for dead sperm whales have been found floating, with no sign of injury or disease save the marks of a submarine battle with the squids, and no doubt many of those which are overcome by their prey never rise to the surface of the sea, but are actually devoured by the very creatures they sought to secure for their own meals. Whalers have known that the sperm whales fed upon cuttlefish for a long time but no one dreamed of the size of the giant squids of the ocean's depths until dead ones were cast upon the beaches of Newfoundland and pieces of their enormous arms were discovered in the stomachs of sperm whale.

Scientists who were interested in the study of these strange monsters of the deep found many of their most interesting specimens in the stomachs of sperm whales and the Prince of Monaco even fitted out an expedition to hunt and kill sperm whales for the sake of the rare specimens of cuttlefish which could be obtained by cutting open the whales. It is owing to their fondness for the squids that the sperm whales produce the rare and valuable substance known as "ambergris." This is a light, porous, greasy material which is at times found floating upon the surface of the sea or cast upon beaches and which is used in making perfumes, not for its scent, but because it possesses the curious property of retaining or absorbing odors to a wonderful degree. It is worth more than its weight in gold and often the whaler who secured a few lumps of ambergris made more money from his find than from all the oil obtained on a long cruise. In former times there was a great deal of mystery surrounding the origin of this strange substance, but bits of cuttlefish beaks were often found in it and it is now known to be a sort of disease growth in the whale's intestines, caused by an accumulation of indigestible portions of the squids, and large quantities are at times secured by dissecting the whales.

Owing to their habit of feeding and the necessity of seeing their prey, sperm whales' eyes are so placed that they can see any object in front of their heads or to either side, but they cannot see to the rear. Unlike the right whales the sperm whales have a terrible weapon of defense in their tooth-armed lower jaw which is capable of biting a whaleboat in two and chewing it into matchwood, and while their great flukes are very powerful they are far less to be dreaded than those of the right whales.

"Beware of a sperm's jaw and a right whale's flukes" is a whaler's maxim always borne in mind and taking advantage of this and the fact that one species can see ahead and the other behind, the whalers strive to approach sperm whales from the rear and right whales directly from the front.

Although the sperm whale has no whalebone, yet its oil is far more valuable than that obtained from the right whales and bowheads and, in addition, this creature furnishes the substance known as "spermaceti," which was formerly among the most valuable of all whale products.

The spermaceti is a clear, limpid, oil-like liquid contained in a great cavity in the sperm whale's head and which is known as the "case;" but upon exposure to the air the spermaceti hardens rapidly and becomes a semi-opaque, wax-like material. It was formerly used in making the best grades of candles and in other arts and manufactures, but has now been largely superseded by stearine and paraffin, just as whale oil has been replaced by petroleum and kerosene.

Very different from the sperm whales, right whales and bowheads are the humpbacks, finbacks and sulfur-bottoms. The finbacks and sulfur-bottoms gave comparatively little oil and bone of inferior quality and were not considered worth taking by the old-time whalers, but today the finback-whale fishery forms a very important industry in Japan, Scandinavia and on our Northwest coast.

One reason that the old whalers left these whales alone was because of the difficulty in securing them. They were among the largest, if not the very largest, of all whales; they were very powerful, rapid swimmers; they were very alert and wary, dangerous when "struck" and they often sank when killed. Today steam whaleships, darting-guns and bombs have made the hunting of finbacks easy and they are kept from sinking by forcing compressed air into their bodies.

The humpbacks, however, were often hunted by the old Yankee whalers and while their oil was inferior to that of the sperm whales they were well worth capturing. As the humpbacks frequented the bays and inlets of the Pacific and Indian Oceans during their breeding season and lived in shallow waters when the cows were accompanied by their calves, the whalers sought them on the coasts of South America, Africa, Madagascar and the islands of the South Seas. This was known as "bay whaling," and compared to arctic or Antarctic whaling, or sperm whaling on the open ocean, it was easy, simple and comparatively safe work.

Although whales were always the main object of the whalers, yet anything which would give oil was taken when opportunity offered and many casks of grampus and porpoise oil were brought home from whaling cruises. Porpoises or "dolphins," as they are often incorrectly called, are found in every sea and while there are many species they are all similar in appearance or habits. Their oil is used for lubricating watches, mathematical instruments and fine machinery and brings a high price, but most of it is obtained from the porpoise fisheries of the Carolina coast and from the Passamaquoddy Indians of Eastport, Maine, who hunt porpoises in canoes. Porpoises are too small, too active and too much trouble to attract the whalers and it was only now and then that they were captured.

Somewhat similar to the porpoises, but much larger and forming a sort of connecting link between them and the true whales, is the grampus, more often known as "blackfish" to the whalers. These creatures go in large schools and are far more sluggish than porpoises and yield a much larger amount of oil. They were often killed by the whalemen, as were also the "white whales" or belugas, a small species of whale, light gray in color and common in the Gulf of St. Lawrence and neighboring waters.

Still another whale-like creature which the whalers at times obtained was the narwhal, or "unicorn whale," a curious, spotted mammal somewhat resembling a porpoise or grampus but with a long, pointed horn or tooth of spirally grooved ivory projecting from the upper jaw, like a great, white pole. The narwhal is an inhabitant of arctic seas, and here in the Far North the whalers also hunted many other animals, such as walrus, seals, bears, muskoxen or in fact anything which produced blubber and oil, which bore hides or skins of value, or which furnished meat which was edible. Indeed some of the arctic whalers were more trappers, hunters and traders than true whalers and found that skins and furs obtained by the friendly Eskimos were more profitable than the whale oil and bone which they ostensibly set out to secure.

Many other whalers sailed to the forbidding and desolate islands of the Antarctic in search: of seals and sea-elephants and at times they spent many months on Kerguelen, South Georgia and other uninhabited, barren and cold spots, while their ships sailed away to Cape Town for repairs and to refit.

The great sea-elephants furnished an enormous quantity of oil and were so stupid and so easily killed that they were almost exterminated by the whalers in many places, but hunting such helpless creatures on land was not true whaling, and the methods by which the slaughter was carried on and the life of the whalers on shore or ice, has nothing to do with their life on shipboard, and seals, sea-elephants or even porpoises deserve no place in the story of the whaler.

3 - HOW THE WHALES WERE CAUGHT

AS ALREADY MENTIONED, the method used in whaling, the outfits required, and the "grounds" to be sought, varied according to the kind of whales to be hunted, but the whalers and whaleships did not confine themselves to any one class of whales, even on a single cruise. Many old whalers were sperm whalers all their lives and never hunted or saw either bowheads or right whales; others never whaled on the open Atlantic or Pacific but sought only the right whales and bowheads of the arctic seas, while some who hunted right whales never killed a bowhead and vice versa.

But as a rule, "all was fish that came to a whaleman's net," figuratively speaking, and whalemen set sail from New Bedford or other ports bound for "any ocean," and before their return, at the end of three, four or five years, hunted sperm whales up and down the wide Atlantic, rounded Cape Horn and hunted whales on the western coast of South America and pushed far into the ice-floes of the Kamchatka seas in search of bowheads. Then, if not filled up, a course was followed down the shores of Japan and through the China Sea; the smoke from their try-works darkened the skies and fouled the spice-laden airs of the Malay Archipelago and Polynesia; they killed humpbacks in the bays of West Africa and Madagascar, and perchance called at Kerguelen ere hoisting topsails for home after thus circumnavigating the globe.

In the early days of New England all the whaling was "shore whaling" by means of small boats and all the whales attacked and captured were those which approached close to the shores and could be seen from the land.

The whales thus obtained were the Biscay whales, a small species of right whale and which has been almost exterminated. The shore whaling was carried on by means of harpoons and lances and a large proportion of the whale men were native American Indians.

In fact the red men were so essential to the success of the early whalers that laws were passed exempting them from many taxes and legal penalties, and the Indian whalemen who enlisted in the army were discharged at the beginning of the whaling season to enable them to take part in the fisheries. Between the first of November and the fifteenth of April, Indians who were whalers were free from lawsuits, arrest for debt or petty offenses, and from military duties, and even after whaling vessels made long sea voyages and shore whaling was practically abandoned the Gay Head and Long Island Indians formed a good portion of the whaling crews. The first sperm whale recorded from Nantucket was taken in 1712, when a whaler, Christopher Hussey,[12] was blown offshore and found himself amid a school of sperm whales. One of these he succeeded in capturing and the gale abating, he towed his prize ashore. This seemingly trivial event was fraught with the greatest importance and led to the establishment of the vast whaling industry and the countless whaleships which made Nantucket famous throughout the world and which paved the way for the wealth and prosperity of other New England town's that depended upon the whalers for their greatest revenue.

The first Nantucket whaling vessels were small, thirty-ton sloops fitted for cruises of a few weeks' duration and after capturing one whale they returned to port. Three years after Christopher Hussey discovered the sperm whales, the value of sperm oil obtained by the Nantucket whalers amounted to over five thousand dollars each season, and within a dozen years a fleet of twenty-five or thirty vessels was engaged in sperm whaling, Nantucket's annual capture of oil was valued at over twenty thousand

[12] Early Nantucket whaleboats were twenty feet long, and manned by a crew of Wampanoag rowers with a single white captain overseeing the oarsmen.

dollars and the little sea-girt Massachusetts island led the world as a whaling port.

These early Nantucket whaleships were very different in size and equipment from the whalers of later years, their methods, implements and appliances were crude, and it was not until 1761 that the oil was even tried out at sea. Once it was discovered that vessels could capture whales, could try out the oil and could store it in casks without returning to port, true deep-water whaling commenced and from that time on, shore whaling was practically abandoned and ocean whaling became an established industry. From the small sloops of early days the vessels were increased in size until large barks, ships and brigs were in almost universal use and were fitted out for cruises of several years' duration.

But the earliest whalers had accomplished much and had adopted the best tools, weapons and implements adapted to the capture and cutting up of whales and the later whalers found it difficult to improve upon the equipment of their predecessors.

For capturing the whales, harpoons or "irons," as the whalemen call them, were used. These were home-made in blacksmith shops and were often rough and crude. The "iron" consists of a slender shank about three feet in length with one end forming a conical recess and the other bearing a pivoted, more or less triangular, blade. To the conical end a heavy oak or hickory pole, six feet in length, is fastened and just below the conical ferrule a stout rope is attached by means of an eye-splice and turn. This line is seized, by marline, at two points on the wooden pole and another eye-splice is formed in the extreme end of the rope. When in use the rope, or line, which is coiled in tubs in the whaleboat, is bent onto the latter eye-splice. The iron is thrown or "darted" into the whale and the pivoted tip, turning at right angles to the shaft, prevents it from being withdrawn and the whale is thus held by the rope attached to the iron shank, and not to the wooden pole.

Many people are under the impression that the iron, or harpoon, is a light, javelin-like affair and is thrown for considerable distances, but as a matter of fact it is a tremendously heavy, clumsy and cumbersome implement and must be "hove" by both hands of the whaleman and cannot be thrown more than fifteen or twenty feet.

The great weight of the harpoon and its stout hickory staff is necessary in order to make the iron penetrate the skin and thick blubber of the whale, and it would require a veritable Hercules to poise one of these irons in one hand and throw it like a javelin for forty or fifty feet, as often depicted in fanciful illustrations of whaling. The harpoon or iron is not intended to kill the whale, but merely to secure a hold upon him and to prevent him from escaping from the boat, but even when "struck" whales often succeed in getting away. The line may break, the iron may pull out or "draw" or may even become twisted and broken off, or the whale may sound or dive beyond the limit of the line and thus compel the whalemen to cut loose in order to save themselves from being drawn below the surface of the sea. Then again the whale may roll over and over, winding the line about his body; he may travel so far that the boat is in danger of being towed out of sight of the ship, or he may turn and ram the boat. If all goes well and the iron holds fast the boat is finally drawn close alongside the stricken monster and he is killed by means of a lance.

The lance formerly used consisted of a slender, iron shank, five or six feet long; with a sharp-pointed, keen-edged, spear-shaped blade. The other end of the shank was conical, like that of the harpoon, and was fitted to a heavy pole about six feet in length. In order to use this instrument the boat had to be hauled within a few feet of the wounded whale and the lance was then driven into his vitals by pushing upon its haft.

This was the most dangerous part of the hunt. Imagine running a frail boat within arm's length of a ninety-foot, wounded whale and actually shoving the lance into his flesh! No wonder many men were killed and injured, numerous boats smashed and many whales lost when accomplishing such a feat. But in later years the bomb-lance largely superseded the old-time weapon and made killing the whales less perilous and more certain.

The bomb-lance most commonly used consisted of an iron or harpoon attached to a pole and beside it a gun-like arrangement containing a brass, steel-tipped dart. The iron was driven or thrown into the whale and when it penetrated

a certain distance a rod came into contact with the whale's skin and this sprung the trigger, discharged the "gun" and drove the heavy dart far into the interior of the whale.

Whale guns and "darting guns" were also invented, some of which were worthless and others practical, but the real old-time Yankee whaleman found the common "iron" and the lance the most satisfactory weapons, and more whales were taken by these simple home-made appliances than by any other means. Nowadays the steam-whaling ships of Japan, Scandinavia and our Northwestern states use gun-harpoons weighing hundreds of pounds and fired from cannon, in order to capture the whales and then kill them by bombs or shells containing an explosive. It is mere slaughter with no element of danger or sport and such whaling is about as uninteresting and unromantic as killing steers in the stockyards of Chicago.

But to return to the methods of the real Yankee whale-men. Once the whale spouted blood and was killed he was towed to the ship and made fast to the starboard or right-hand side by means of a chain around the small (the narrow portion of the body where it joins the tail or flukes), with the tail near the bow of the ship and the head under the gangway – an opening in the ship's bulwarks between the foremast and mainmast and the process of cutting-in or securing the blubber commenced.

Although, the method of cutting-in or cutting, as the whalers say, varied somewhat according to the species of whale, the principle was the same in every case and the method used in cutting in a sperm whale will serve as an example.

The main difference between cutting in a sperm and a right whale lies in the details of handling the head, the entire head of the sperm being taken in, whereas in the case of the right whale the bone is removed and taken aboard.

As soon as the whale is alongside under the cutting-stage (a frail platform of planks swung over the vessel's side), a hole is cut through the blubber between the eye and fin at the point A on the illustration and in this a huge, iron hook, known as the blubber-hook, is inserted by one of the boat-steerers who is lowered in a bowline to the whale's carcass. Deep cuts are then made through the blubber at each side and across the end of the blanket-piece, as shown at C-D and C-F, and by means of a tackle attached to the blubber-hook the piece of blubber is torn from the whale's body and the creature is rolled over by the strain until it rests upon its side. Next a cut is made between the upper jaw and the portion of the head known as the junk, as shown by the line L-C, and if the whale is very large, another cut is made between the junk and case, as at B-E, and still another from E-F. An incision is also made across the root of the lower jaw, from the corner of the mouth to G; a chain is then attached to the lower jaw, as shown at H, and this is hooked or shackled to the second-cutting tackle and is raised while the tackle attached to A is slacked off, thus causing the whale's body to roll over on its back. Then by hauling on the jaw-tackle and cutting through the end of the tongue and the flesh, the lower jaw is separated from the head and is hoisted on deck. The first tackle, attached to the loose piece of blubber at A, is then hauled up by a windlass until the whale is turned completely over and cuts are made from L to C, from E to F and from B to E on the opposite side of the head. Close to the jaw at the point I a hole is cut through the junk; another is made at J and a third at K and to these "straps" and lines are made fast. The second cutting-tackle is then hooked to the strap at I, the fluke-chain is slacked off, and the tackle to A is lowered, and by hoisting away on the head tackle the carcass is raised to an almost vertical position.

From the cutting-stage men with spades (sharp-edged, square-ended knives at the ends of long poles) hack away at the spot between the jaw and junk C-L until the gash made is opened by the weight of the body. Then the root of the case from E-F is cut away, the junk and case or head are freed from the body and jaw and the great mass is fastened temporarily to the vessel's quarter.

In some cases, however, the head is twisted from the body. By placing a stout, oak stave with one end resting against the ship's side and the other in a recess cut in the side of the head, and by hauling on the blubber-tackle the body is turned and the head wrenched off. When the head is clear the fluke-chain is hauled in until the whale lies alongside the ship: and the men commence stripping off the blubber. By cutting spirally around the body with the spades and by hauling on the blubber-hook tackle fastened to A, the blanket-piece is rolled or unwound from the body until the small is reached when the tail is cut off and the rear end of the body is hoisted on board. This method is used when the head is too large to hoist on deck.

As fast as the blubber, or blanket-piece, is taken from the whale it is lowered into the hatch and placed black skin down in the blubber-room where the men cut the mass of blubber into horse-pieces or chunks about fourteen inches square. These pieces are then taken on deck and are passed forward to the mincing horse where they are minced by means of two-handled, cleaver-like knives or by a mincing machine.

Meanwhile the fires in the try-works[13] are started with shavings and wood and the minced horse-pieces are placed in the great iron kettles to boil. As soon as the oil fills the kettles, it is ladled into the cooler and then into waiting casks, which are set aside to cool and are later stored below. The fires are fed by the scraps or cracklings from which the oil has been boiled out and, if at night, pieces of blubber are burned in the bug light (an open iron frame) to light the scene with its weird glare. When the blanket-piece has been tried out the junk or head blubber is cut up and tried separately, for this furnishes oil of a superior quality and is far more valuable than the body oil.

The work of cutting-in and boiling is the hardest labor the whalers are called upon to perform and there is no lull in the activity and ceaseless toil while boiling is in progress. The boiling watch is of six hours' duration with half the crew on duty and while the officers (mates and boat-steerers) attend to the pots and fires and ladle out the oil some of the men are busy in the blubber-room, at the mincing horse or machine; others are sweating away storing the casks of oil, while one man is always at the wheel and another is constantly on lookout at the masthead.

The hardest work of all was that of the crew who manned the windlass and tackles, for whalers had no labor-saving devices and the huge tackle-blocks were old-fashioned, worn and seldom greased and whaling skippers seemed to delight in watching the men toil and apparently used every endeavor to make their work as hard and exhausting as possible. Moreover, the process of cutting-in and boiling is inexpressibly dirty, nauseating work and how any human beings could stand it – much less choose it as a means of livelihood – is almost beyond

---

[13] Brick fireplaces on deck near the foremast.

comprehension. Slipping on the blubber-strewn deck, drenched with oil and grimed with soot, the work was bad enough, but the worst part came later, after the real cutting-in and boiling were over.

The great lower jaws were left on deck until the gums rotted and allowed the teeth to be stripped from the bone, for the teeth were prized for carving and scrimshaw work by the crew and were divided among the men, and the stench of the decaying meat as it laid upon the deck beneath a tropical sun may better be imagined than described.

Still worse were the casks of fat lean. The fat-leans are those portions of the blubber stripped from the horse-pieces and which have fragments of flesh adhering to them and these were thrown into open casks and left to rot, for the sake of the oil which drained from them during decomposition. After they had become thoroughly decayed the waste material was removed by the men who were compelled to fish out the putrid meat with their hands and in order to do this they were obliged to lean inside the casks and to inhale the noisome fumes and terrible stench of the awful mass for hours at a time.

But when at last the three or four days' unceasing labor was completed, the oil casks had been stored below, and the decks had been cleared up and washed down, the tired men had the time to themselves. All work ceased, save that absolutely necessary in handling the ship, and the members of the crew amused themselves by carving whales' teeth, making scrimshaw work or mending clothes until the cry of "There she blows" aroused all hands and everything was cast aside in preparation for the coming chase with its attendant perils, hardships and weary days of heart-breaking toil.

4 - WHALING SHIPS AND THEIR CREWS

STAUNCH, SEAWORTHY AND "ABLE" as they were, yet the old Yankee whaleships were neither graceful nor beautiful vessels. Speed, comfort and appearance were of no importance and the ships were heavy, bluff-bowed and "tubby." Of course there were exceptions, some of the whaling ships were the equals of any of the famous "clippers" for speed and graceful lines and were kept in the pink of condition, with standing rigging taut and well tarred, paint bright and fresh.

But the majority were slipshod, dingy, weather-beaten; bearing scars of countless battles with wind and sea, reeking with oil and grease and smelling to high Heaven. The old saying that a sailor can "smell a whaler twenty miles to windward" is scarcely an exaggeration. Betwixt catching, killing, cutting-in and boiling, the whalemen found little time to keep their vessels ship-shape. There were stove boats to be repaired, irons to be made, poles to be fitted, lines to be spliced, bent and coiled down, rowlocks to be "thumbed," straps to be made, knives, spades irons and lances to be sharpened and a thousand and one other duties to be attended to. What rest the crews had was well earned and in order that the men should be fresh and able to fulfill their duties they were allowed the time between one boiling and the next chase for their own amusement and recreation.

As long as the ship held together and was able to weather the seas and gales, as long as it would carry its cargo of oil and bone, as long as the patched and dingy sails would serve to catch the winds and carry the whalers hither and thither, the whalemen were satisfied, and some of the old hulks, which were used for whaling, would appear fit only for the scrap-pile to a merchant sailor.

I have seen whaling ships laid up in New Bedford and New London with grass and weeds growing from the crevices of their planking and yet a short time later these same ramshackle old craft were fitted out for long cruises and braved the storms and stress of the Arctic and Antarctic oceans and, strangest of all, returned safely to port full of oil. When after whales it mattered not if yard-long seaweeds bedecked the ships' bottoms or if halyards, braces or falls were rotten and parted at a touch – the growths could be cleaned off at the end of the cruise and rigging could be patched and spliced. As long as whales could be caught, and until the hold could contain no more oil, the whale-men kept to the broad oceans and when at last they sailed, fully laden, into the harbors of their home ports, they looked more like the *Flying Dutchman* or the ghosts of ancient wrecks than seaworthy ships manned by crews of flesh and blood.

But if the whaleships sailed into port weed-grown, storm-beaten, patched and forlorn, as great change was wrought in them ere the capstan-pawls clanked and the men's chanteys echoed across the waters as they weighed anchors and manned sheets and braces outward bound. Rapidly the oil-filled casks were hoisted from the hold, spars and upper rigging were sent down, decks were cleared and soon the great, empty hulk rose high and light beside the dock. By means of gigantic blocks and tackle the hull was hove-down, exposing the ship's bottom and men standing on planks and rafts worked busily, cleaning off the accumulation of sea growths, repairing plates, caulking and overhauling. Top-sides were cleaned and painted; standing rigging was renewed, tarred-down and tightened; spars were scraped and sent aloft; new sails were bent on; old running rigging was replaced; and in a short time the ship was once more fresh, bright, spick-and-span and ready to refit for another cruise.

Few people have any conception of the number of supplies and the variety of articles required in fitting out a whaling ship for a cruise. Aside from the necessary equipment which had to do directly with whaling, there were supplies for the men, ship's stores, trade goods, tools, and a vast number of incidentals, the whole totaling some 650 different articles. The ship was really a floating department store, carpenter shop, blacksmith shop, shipyard and several other things all rolled into one. But it was essential that the whalers should carry a very large number of stores which would never be needed on a merchant ship, for aside from the articles required in whaling it was necessary that a whaling vessel should be able to make any repairs needed on ship or boats for three years or more. As a rule, they cruised in out-of-the-way spots where supplies, tools or other articles could not be purchased and the whalemen therefore set sail prepared for any emergency and equipped to be absolutely independent of the rest of the world for years at a time.

When we stop to realize that nearly one hundred whaleships were often fitting out at New Bedford (and at other ports also) at one time, we can understand what the whaling industry meant to the New England ports. The tremendous quantities of goods purchased by the whalers is well shown by the following list of supplies furnished the New Bedford fleet of sixty-five vessels for the season of 1858:

13,650 bls. flour
13,000 bu. Beans
39,000 lbs. rice
32,500 lbs. codfish
16,300 lbs. ham
1,300 bu. Onions
26,000 bu. Potatoes
1,000,000 staves
260 cords of pine
52,000 lbs. copper nails
15,000 lbs. sheath nails

32,500 ft. boat boards
65,000 ft. pine boards
200 casks lime
205,000 yds. Canvas
130,000 lbs. tobacco
97,500 gals. Molasses
5,200 lbs. linseed oil
78,000 lbs. butter
13,000 lbs. paint
1,950 bu. Corn
120 casks powder
1,200 cords oak wood
19,500 bu, salt
520,000 lbs. copper
19,500 lbs. cheese
739,000 lbs. cordage
13,300 lbs. raisins
22,500 lbs. flags
32,500 bbls. Water
234,000 yds. cotton clot
33,000 tons rivets
39,000 gals. white lead
450 whaleboats
400 gals. Turpentine
23,000 bricks
1,000 gals. Liquors
7,150 bbls. Pork
10,400 bbls. Beef
78,000 lbs. sugar
39,000 bbls. Apples
14,300 lbs. tea
18,000 Ibs. Coffee
2,000 lbs. candles
400 bbls. Vinegar
1,000 tons hoop iron
260,000 ft. heading
36,000 ft. oars

400 bbls. Tar
13,000 lbs. cotton twine
8,500 iron poles
2,600 gals. Rum
260 bbls. Meal

As these alone meant an outlay of nearly two million dollars it can be seen how much the tradesmen and artisans of such towns as New Bedford were benefited by the whalers and aside from the actual cash placed in circulation, a vast army of workmen, manufacturers and skilled laborers was built up, all of whom were dependent upon the whaleships for their livelihood. There were thousands of barrels and casks to be made, countless irons, lances and spades to be forged, hundreds of sails to be sewn, and innumerable boats to be built, as well as an endless number of other articles necessary to the whalemen and which could be made at the home port far better and more cheaply than elsewhere.

Even newspapers and periodicals were published in which not a line or word was printed which did not relate to the whalers or was not of interest to the whalemen and their families and friends. Their pages contained advertisements of outfitters, ship-chandlers, dealers in nautical supplies, and similar tradesmen; there were quotations of exchange, the prices of oil and bone and pilotage fees; there were columns devoted to news from far-distant parts of the world reporting arrivals, departures, wrecks and catches of whaleships and, most important of all, were lists giving the names of all the whaling vessels of the Atlantic coast, their tonnage, captains and agents; when they sailed, where they were bound, where they had been spoken and the amount of oil they had taken.

In many a New England town "whale was king" in those days and the life, business, commerce – in fact the very existence of New Bedford and many other ports –

depended entirely upon the whaling industry. Whole forests were leveled and great sawmills were established to furnish lumber, boards, staves and cordwood. Huge sail-lofts were kept constantly filled with busy workmen. Long rope-walks were built and nothing but cordage for whaleships made therein. Dozens of forges glowed from morn till night and hammer rang incessantly on anvil as irons, lances and blubber-hooks were forged by the toiling smiths. Boat-builders worked feverishly to keep the ships supplied with boats. Coopers toiled early and late making casks for oil. Clay banks were dug away and great kilns were erected solely to make bricks for the ships' try-works. Looms clicked and thousands of spindles whirred to make canvas, cotton and bunting for the whalemen. The crops of entire farms were raised to furnish the provisions for the whalers. Herds of cows were required to furnish the butter and cheese. The docks were piled high, the warehouses packed full with whalers' stores, and an endless procession of trucks and drays toiled creaking over the cobbled, waterfront streets, laden with boxes, bales and barrels, all to go forth over untold leagues of sea in whaleships' holds.

Moreover, each and every workman, laborer or artisan did his best to produce results worthy of his name and that of New Bedford, or the town wherein he labored. Each took a personal pride in the success of the whalers and their catch; each knew that upon his individual skill, his honest labor, and the quality of his work depended the very lives of his fellows, and each put his whole heart and soul into what he did.

The cooper knew that his casks must be tight and strong to hold the precious oil in safety during many months and in all sorts of weather. The blacksmith realized that upon the temper of his steel depended the capture or loss of the whales. The sail-maker knew that the canvas he stitched must withstand long weeks of drenching rain, months of broiling sun and gales of hurricane force. The rope-maker was aware that if his lines parted the stricken whale would escape, but of them all none worked with greater care, none exhibited so much skill, and none produced such perfect results as the makers of the whaleboats.

To the whalemen the boats were of primary importance. In them the actual hunt took place, upon the boats' strength, lightness and ease of handling their lives hung and never did the boat-builders fail them. Through long years of whaling the boats had been developed until practical perfection was reached and never yet has a boat been built which for speed, staunchness, seaworthiness and "handiness" excels the whaleboats of the Massachusetts whalemen.

Thirty feet in length and six feet wide, with a depth of twenty-two inches amidship and thirty-seven inches at the bow and stern, the whaleboats seem mere cockleshells to one who is not familiar with them; but these tiny craft can ride the heaviest seas, can withstand the hardest gales, and can resist the most terrific strains with perfect safety.

They are pulled by five great oars measuring fourteen, sixteen and eighteen feet in length, or are sailed by a simple spritsail, and are steered by a twenty-two-foot steering oar. The bow- and-tub-oars of sixteen feet are used on one side and pull against the fourteen-foot harpooners and after-oars and the midship oar on the other side, and propelled by these and the straining muscles of five men the boats fairly leap through the water. In their equipment the boats are as perfect as in their model and construction and each article has its own place and is always where it belongs. If an iron were mislaid, if a lance were out of reach, if a line kinked or if a hatchet were not at hand, six lives might pay the penalty for someone's carelessness.

Near the bow, and resting in their cleats with keen tips sheathed are the irons and lances – two live irons, two or three spares, and two or three lances – all ready to the boat-steerer's or mate's hand. In wooden tubs are coiled the beautifully laid lines of finest hemp – three hundred fathoms in length. A hatchet to cut the line in case of need is in the bow-box; a water keg is lashed in its chocks; there are candles, a compass, lanterns, glasses and matches in lockers at the stern; a boathook, waif-flags, fluke-spades and canvas buckets are all in their appointed places, and paddles are at hand for approaching the whale silently when oars cannot be used.

In the boat's stem is a deep slot to receive the line; at the stern is a stout post or loggerhead over which a turn of the line is taken when the whale is fast; the rowlocks are carefully thumbed with greased marline to prevent the rattle, or squeal of oars, and in the forward thwart is the clumsy cleat or knee brace in which the whaleman rests his leg when throwing the iron at his quarry. Such are the boats used by the whalers and each ship carried several. Owing to the broad gangway in the starboard side of the ships only one boat is carried on the great wooden davits on the quarter of that side while the three others – if a four-boat ship – are slung to the davits on the port or larboard side. In addition, two extra boats are stored on overhead racks between the main and mizzen masts where they serve to cast a shade and to shelter the cabin.

When at last the boats are in their places, the stores, provisions and equipment are aboard, and the ship is ready for sea, there is little room to spare aboard a whaler. In the forecastle the crew are quartered; in the forehold are spare rigging, hawsers, cutting-in gear and tackles, spare lumber, oars, anchors and similar things, and the main hold is filled with casks. To economize space these contain the supplies, provisions, dry goods, trade goods, clothing and water for the cruise. Those of the lowest tier contain the water, others are filled with tins of bread and food, others with miscellaneous articles and those of the topmost tier hold the things which will be used before the first whales are taken, so that when the grounds are reached the casks will be empty and ready for use.

Every available niche and corner is full, the ship is as deeply laden as though a freighter with full cargo, and when at last the final bale and bag is on board, and the full complement of men has been shipped, the whaleship is ready for her long cruise to the uttermost parts of the globe; perhaps to return fully laden in a few months, perhaps to cruise under tropic suns and through fields of ice for year after year, perchance never to return – sunk, no one knows when or where – one of that great fleet of "missing ships" whose fate is never learned.

But what of the whalemen themselves? Without them the vast quantities of supplies would be useless, the carefully fashioned implements, weapons and equipment would be of no worth, the boats, perfect as they are, could not be used, and no whale could be captured, no oil obtained, and no cruise made.

The personnel of an average whaling ship consisted of thirty-five or forty men whose ratings were as follows: captain or "skipper;" four mates or "officers;" four boat-steerers; a cooper; a steward; a cabin-boy; a cook; four ship-keepers, or "spare-men," and four boats' crews of four men each, or sixteen "seamen," besides an extra boy or two, a blacksmith and a carpenter, who were often carried.

The duties of each man were definite, and every member of the ship's company knew his duty and performed it without question or hesitation. Each boat was in charge of a mate with its crew of four oarsmen and a boat-steerer and at times the captain took charge of a boat or lowered for a whale and in that case he took the fourth mate's boat and the latter officer acted as the captain's boat-steerer. The men in each boat were assigned to specific places and aside from pulling the boat they had other duties to perform. Thus the bow-oar was the place of honor and the man who pulled this oar was the mate's right-hand man and assisted the officer with the lances when killing. The midship was the longest and heaviest oar and the midship oarsman had little to do save pull on his huge sweep. The "tub-oarsman threw water on the line to prevent it from burning as it ran rapidly out when the whale sounded, while the stroke-oarsman furnished the stroke to the other men and also aided the boat-steerer in keeping the line clear and in hauling in slack and coiling it down.

The first or "harpooner's oar," as it was called, was pulled by the boat-steerer when going on a whale until fairly near the creature. The boat-steerer then laid his oar aside and took his place at the boat's bow and "struck" the whale with his iron, while the mate steered the craft with the huge steering-oar. Once fast the mate and boat-steerer changed places, the latter taking charge of the steering oar and becoming the boat-steerer in fact as well as name, while the mate took his position in the bow, to kill the whale.

When the boats were away the ship, under shortened canvas, was left in charge of the captain (if he did not "lower"), the four spare-men or ship-keepers, the cook, steward, boys and cooper. Aboard the ship, when cruising, the crew or seamen had little to do, once they were on the grounds, save to swing the yards, trim sail or perform other work necessary in navigating the vessel; for every ounce of strength and every spark of vitality was conserved to be brought into instant use when a whale was sighted and the chase commenced.

When on the grounds each boat's crew formed a watch, thus dividing the night into four watches of three hours each – if the vessel were a four-boat ship. Unlike the merchant sailors to whom eight-bell watches are almost sacred, the whalemen commenced them watches at six bells, and in this respect they differed from all other sea-men. Thus the first watch was from 7 until 11 P.M.; the middle watch was from 11 until 3, and the last watch was from 3 until 7 A.M. Moreover, half-hours were never struck on a whaling vessel's bell, only the even hours be-ing sounded, and one, three, five or seven strokes never rang across the waters from a whaleship.

At sunset the lighter sails were taken in, the topsails were reefed, and the ship was hove close into the wind with sails set, so she would remain nearly stationary and by occasionally "wearing ship" the vessel would be at practically the same spot at daybreak as on the preceding evening. This does not apply to the arctic whaling ships, however, for in high latitudes – where it was light throughout the night – whaling was carried on during the whole twenty-fours hours; in fact the first right whale taken in the Arctic was killed at midnight.

In the daytime four men were kept constantly at the mastheads, two men forward and a mate and boat-steerer at the main, on the lookout for whales, and the ship would tack with long stretches to windward and would then sail down before the wind, thus covering nearly every square mile of the cruising ground. But for the first few months of the cruise the men had far from an easy time and were compelled to labor from dawn until dark, as well as during the night watches; for there was general overhauling to be done, decks to be scoured, odds and ends to be stowed and, most important and hardest of all, the "green hands" to be broken in and trained. It may seem strange to think of "breaking in" a whaler's crew until we learn who and what the men were, for despite popular ideas and storybook tales the whalemen were never sailors.

The old-time Yankee skippers were seamen – and wonderfully skillful and proficient seamen at that – as were the officers or mates, and the boat-steerers were practiced, skilled and efficient hands; but the crew, or so-called "seamen" – the men who furnished the sinew and muscle, the men who performed the hardest labor, the common soldiers of the army of whalemen – were "greenies."

Derelicts of humanity from the gutters, raw-boned lads from the interior farms, ne'er-do-wells of respectable families, factory hands, clerks, vagabonds, gamblers, tramps, criminals striving to evade the law, loafers from park benches – they formed a motley crew culled from far and near, and classed under the common appellation of "bums" by the officers and shippers.

Some lured by the expectation of easily earned wealth; others thinking to find romance and adventure in the whaleman's calling; still others hunted from place to place and seeking the deck of a whaler and the wide seas as their only refuge, and still more drugged, filled with vile liquor and shanghaied, they shipped as "seamen" on the vessels "bound to any seas" for any length of time, only to find themselves penniless, helpless, veritable slaves, whose master was the skipper with power beyond that of any king, their drivers the mates and their home the kennel-like fo'c'stle.

Of true deep-water sailors there was no dearth in the ports from which the whalers sailed, but such men were not wanted on the whaling ships. Shippers and captains, owners and agents avoided the real seamen as they would the plague – they would not take them for love or money if it could be avoided and, as one captain remarked they wouldn't "ship a real sailor if he paid his passage."

The reason for this strange state of affairs is obvious, if we consider the means and methods by which the crews were obtained, the way they were treated, the work they were called upon to perform, and the actual earnings of the whalemen.[14]

The crews were obtained through shipping offices with headquarters at New Bedford, or some other port, and with agents scattered here and there at the principal cities, especially in the Middle West and the interior of New England.

---

[14]   Author note: Whalemen never worked at regular wages, but were employed on "lays," or in other words, the ship's articles provided that each man should receive the proceeds of one barrel of oil out of a certain definite number. The division of the lays varied with different ships and in different years; the men and officers being satisfied with smaller lays in the early years of whaling, when oil was high, than in later years when the price fell. Just how the lays were apportioned and the amounts the members of the crew received as their shares from a cruise may be seen from the following examples: one of which shows the lays of a ship sailing in 1807; the other in 1860.

By means of lurid, attractive advertisements and circulars these men drew the future whalemen to their net. They were promised a lay of the ship's catch – in other words, one barrel of oil out of a certain number – an advance of seventy-five dollars, an outfit of clothes, board and lodging, until aboard ship; and glorious verbal pictures were painted of the easy life led, the enormous profits made and the strange lands visited on a whaling cruise.

As fast as the men were gathered in they were sent to the port, where they were taken in charge by the resident agent and were placed in the cheapest and foulest of boarding-houses and were furnished with a so-called "outfit" of the shoddiest and most worthless sort. For each man secured, the shipper received ten dollars, in addition to all the expenses incidental to the transportation, board and outfit, and as this was not forthcoming until the men were aboard ship and at sea the shippers saw to it that the men were on hand when the anchor was hoisted.

But what of the advance of seventy-five dollars promised, to each of the unfortunate men? From this imaginary amount were deducted all the expenses which the shipper defrayed, as well as the ten dollars head payment, and every article furnished, every item charged, was doubled, trebled or quadrupled by the rascally outfitters. An outfit costing five dollars at the most was charged to the men at twenty-five dollars, the tariff of the small boats for carrying the men from the dock to the ship was doubled, the train fares were falsified, the boarding-house rates exaggerated, and when at last the account was presented and "signed off" by the poor, deluded, embryo whaleman he had not a cent of his promised advance coming to him. Of course none but green hands, men absolutely inexperienced in the ways of the sea and of whalers, would submit to this sort of treatment or would calmly accept the shoddy outfits and the outfitters' bills without a protest. No Jack Tar could be fooled, robbed and bamboozled in this way, and for this reason shippers and captains alike fought shy of the real seaman with his knowledge of "sharks" and their ways.

This, however, was not the only reason why the whalers preferred the "bums" and farmers' boys to true sailors. A seaman might ship as a whaler with his eyes open or he might be shanghaied and once at sea he might submit to the whaler's treatment and life, but at the first port he would desert and long before a foreign shore was reached he would make his presence and his dissatisfaction felt.

Jack at best is a grumbler; he knows just how far his superiors can go; he knows what he is entitled to, the duties he is supposed to perform; and among the riff-raff crew he would be sure to stir up discontent, trouble – mutiny, perhaps – and would become the leader, the dominant feature and the trouble-breeder of the crew. But by themselves the green hands were helpless and would stand almost anything without danger of causing trouble. Suspicious of one another, equally green and cowed by the officers, they were incapable of organized resistance. They had no one to whom they could look to as a leader, they knew nothing of their rights, and everyone distrusted and disliked his fellows.

This spirit the officers fostered and encouraged, for as long as the men hated one another there was little fear of a concerted uprising and any plots or plans made were sure to be reported by some member of the company. In one respect, however, the men of the crew were in perfect accord – they all hated and detested the mates, although fearing and obeying them. Even the danger of desertion was so minimized as to be unworthy of a thought. The men were penniless, they were not sailors, and in most cases had no trade or occupation with which to keep soul and body together if they left the ship. In a foreign port they would be worse off than on the sea, for they were ignorant of the languages, they could not ship on another vessel, and they did not even know that they could appeal to a consul to be sent home as distressed seamen and even if they did so, they were in fear of the results when they reached the States. True sailors, on the other hand, would have no such difficulties, and the few that were now and then shipped – usually by accident – left the vessels at the first port at which the whalers called. Oftener than not the officers were glad to be well rid of them, and many a desertion was suggested by the captain or his mates who handed a few bills to an undesirable member of the crew and hinted that he would not be missed until the vessel was on the high seas.

But the whalemen who ship on the few whaling vessels that sail from New Bedford today are mainly men of a different sort – Portuguese from the Azores or the Cape Verde Islands – many of them nearly full-blooded negroes and black as ebony, but hard working, industrious and good whalers. These men "know the ropes," they are well able to look out for themselves, and are far too experienced, too wise and too "canny," as a Scotchman would say, to be misled, robbed or cheated by the sharpest shark or outfitter that ever disgraced New Bedford's waterfront with his presence. Even the captains of today are mostly Portuguese and many of the vessels are Portuguese-owned, for the natives of the Western Islands are satisfied with smaller profits, can live more cheaply, and are more thrifty than their American predecessors. While they are often sadly lacking in a knowledge of seamanship and some of them cannot even "throw a half-hitch around a spile," as an old sailor expressed it, yet the Portuguese skippers are skillful whalers, good businessmen, strict disciplinarians and secure catches which would make the old-time Yankee whalemen turn green with envy.

Perchance the reader may wonder why the whalemen made no complaint upon their return to their home port or why societies or others took no interest in their welfare; why the laws were never invoked in their behalf and how the whalers were able to secure crews after their methods became known. The explanation is simple and herein lies still another reason why real sailors were not welcomed on the whaling ships.

In the first place the same men never shipped twice and thus took little or no interest in the treatment of future crews. Moreover, they were not "seamen" within the meaning of the law or as interpreted by the sailors' aid societies, and thus had no redress from such sources. Many of them were fugitives from justice and were only too anxious to drop out of sight and keep clear of the law, while the large majority were so heartily sick of the sea and all connected with it that they counted themselves lucky once more to step on to dry land and betake themselves to the park benches, the farms or the mills from which they had come-wiser if poorer men, their "lay" exhausted by "shore money," tobacco and calls upon the "slop-chest;" their sole possessions a ticket from the port to their home town and a few patched and ragged clothes.

Once in a great while some man shipped time after time with the whalers, despite the robberies and falsehoods of the outfitters and the hardships of the life at sea and old New Bedford whalemen tell an amusing story of one such character. This man, a typical vagrant whose only resting place is a bench on Boston's Common, has appeared annually for fifteen years to ship as a whaleman from New Bedford but no sooner does his ship reach Fayal[15] than he deserts. For a few months he lives an indolent, easy life in the Azores, then he appeals to the American consul, is shipped home "like a bloomin' lord" as he expresses it and again resumes his life at the "Hub" until the next whaling season.

Occasionally, too, some unfortunate, who had been robbed, man-handled and deceived, bided his time and vented all his pent-up feelings and anger upon the rascally men who had sold him into servitude. One such man

---

[15] Fayal, also spelled Faial, is the one of the central Azorean islands.

returned after a long cruise, spent his last cent on a re-volver and cartridges, walked into the office of the shark who had shipped him and shot the fellow dead. Justifiable as the act may have been, the whaler paid the penalty of the law for his crime, but for a long time thereafter the sharks kept themselves in seclusion and were more honest in their dealings. It was a wholesome lesson and the great pity is that it was not taught more often.

5 - OUTWARD BOUND

WHEN THE LAST SUPPLIES and stores were stowed, the last of the green hands had been shipped, and the captain and mates had said their last farewells and had come aboard, the anchor was weighed, sails were sheeted home, and the whaler slipped past the harbor lights – outward bound. With the shores of New England a mere blur on the horizon astern, the long swell of the Atlantic rolling under their keel, and the ocean wind humming in the rigging, the real life of the whalemen commenced.

Little did the landlubber crew dream of what was in store for them, but they were not long kept in ignorance, for as soon as the ships were on the "high seas" the training of the crew began. Deathly seasick, filled with terror and dread at every lurch or roll of the ship, thrown hither and thither by the heaving deck, dazed and confused by their strange surroundings and faint with dizziness each time they looked upward at the soaring, lofty trucks, the greenies were ordered into the rigging.

Encouraged by curses, spurred on by the sharp point of a marlinspike or a rope's end the trembling wretches usually managed to crawl for a few feet up the ratlines. It was a case of necessity, for those who failed received kicks or blows and were glad to choose the lesser of two evils and trust to the perilous shrouds rather than to the mercy of the officers. But "needs must when the devil drives" as the old saying goes and no devil ever drove more relentlessly than a Yankee whaler mate and within a wonderfully short time after leaving port the former vagabonds, farmers and what not were able to go aloft, man the yards and even keep a lookout from the to'gallant cross-trees. Some were far more proficient than others and readily learned the rigging, ropes and sails, but others were hopeless and never learned to distinguish the main-brace from the sheets or a halyard from a backstay, despite every effort of the mates to pound knowledge into their heads with a belaying-pin.

But if they couldn't become able seamen they could learn to pull a boat, and whenever the sea was smooth and the wind light the boats were lowered and the men were drilled in handling them. Of course, their first efforts with the cumbersome oars were ludicrous, for they had never seen or touched an oar before, but practice will make perfect in almost any profession and no one knew better how to teach men to handle boats than the mates and boat-steerers of the whaling ships.

Very soon the men could handle the long oars and could pull in unison; and a keen rivalry springing up between the different boats' crews, the men put heart and soul into this work and became splendid oarsmen, capable of lifting the whaleboats across the seas for hour after hour or pulling towards a whale as silently as ghosts.

From dawn to dark the training was kept up without intermission for the first four or five months or until the "grounds" were reached, but quite often – in fact, as a usual thing, this first part of the voyage was broken by a call at the Azores or the Cape Verde Islands.

Here a few native Portuguese were sometimes shipped and quantities of fresh fruits, vegetables and supplies were secured. These, known to whalers as "recruits," were divided among the men and if the captain saw fit members of the crew were sometimes given shore leave.

When at last the ships squared away from the Western islands the cruise really commenced and often for years at a time the whalers never touched again at a civilized port, for their search for whales carried them to the uttermost parts of the earth, and the farther they went from the frequented seas the more likelihood there was of finding good grounds. Voyages of three or four years were common; many ships were gone five, six, or more years and one well-known captain stated that he had spent only seventeen months at home during fifteen years.

On such long voyages, thousands of miles from home, far from the restraint of law or civilization and by law and custom absolutely supreme in power, it is little wonder that many of the captains and mates reverted to barbarism and brutality. Of course, many of the skippers and their officers were decent, humane, law abiding and kind-hearted, and treated their crews like human beings. Still other captains were sanctimonious to a degree, and the loneliness of their lives, the mystery of the trackless sea and the ever-present menace of death, unbalanced their minds. Becoming monomaniacs on religion, they endangered their ships and men by their acts while under the spell of their delusions, and often ended their careers by committing suicide. Far too many, however, were naturally brutal, calloused, hard-drinking men and while they kept themselves under reasonable control when at home they threw their masks aside, once they were on the high seas, and appeared in their true forms of fiends incarnate.

The life of the common seaman was bad enough on a whaler under the best of conditions and one can well imagine what it must have been when left to the tender mercies of a captain and mates who devoted their spare moments to devising new deviltries to practice on their helpless men. Now and again the tales of their inhuman acts reached the authorities at home or abroad and the brutes were arrested and tried, but the word of a common whaleman carried little weight against that of a captain or his officers and money from the ship's owners was always forthcoming to purchase the acquittal of skippers or mates thus haled to court.

The tortures and cruelties which some of these men inflicted upon their crews are almost incredible and yet they are beyond dispute and are borne out by entries in journals and logbooks, the records of courts; and the reports of consuls and other reliable men. One captain was wont to amuse himself by sending the men aloft and taking pot-shots at them with his revolver. Others strung the men up by their thumbs for hours at a time for the most trivial offenses and one well-known captain, who still lives in New Bedford, caused one of the crew to be stripped and scrubbed with a brick and lye daily. This terrible torture drove the victim mad and while the captain escaped unscathed (he is mild and gentle enough today) he came far too near the shadow of State's prison and the gallows for comfort.

These are but a few instances culled at random and scores of other cases, fully as bad or even worse, might be mentioned. Moreover, such inconceivably brutal and inhuman acts are not all confined to the past. Hardly a season goes by without complaints of unbearable cruelty and even murder being made, and while these are usually hushed up, once in a while they are brought to the attention of the public.

Only a few weeks ago the mate of a New Bedford whaling schooner complained that the captain had gagged him by a belaying-pin[16] forced into his mouth and tied by rope around his head and that in this condition he had been confined for a long time. If skippers still treat their officers in such a manner we can imagine the treatment their crews receive and of which the world never hears.

As a rule, however, the men probably fared far better and were treated with more humanity than they were accustomed to when ashore. The hard knocks they received, the miserable food they ate, and the filthy work they were obliged to perform, while appearing awful to people of refinement and sensibilities, were of little moment to the hardened, vicious and dissipated wretches who composed the bulk of whaleships' crews.

To a vagrant who is accustomed to being roused from drunken slumber by a policeman's club, a rope's end or

---

[16] Rod used to secure rope.

even a belaying-pin is scarcely more than a caress. To one who has toiled at building stone walls or plowing a rocky New England farm, heaving on a windlass or tailing onto a tackle is child's play. To the waif who picks his living from the garbage of the slums, the worm-eaten biscuit and the rotten meat of the whaleship is welcome fare; and to him whose life ashore is constantly menaced by a stone cell or the hangman's noose anything is bearable as long as the law cannot reach him.

We should not waste too much sympathy on the whalemen, for the majority richly deserved all they received and despite their rough life, their abuse, their miserable fare and their ill-treatment, the one-time "bums" became brave, efficient and hard workers – at least while aboard ship. Whaling was a hard school and the whaling captains were severe teachers, but they turned out men from mighty raw material and what they had to endure, the difficulties they were compelled to face, and the obstacles they overcame will never be known or appreciated.

Until the "grounds" were reached the whaleman's life was one of constant drudgery, endless tasks and incessant training, but once in the region where whales were likely to be found, every attention was given solely to the expected chase. From their lofty station on the to'gallant crosstrees, the lookouts scan the sea, watching with straining eyes to catch the faint blur of vapor which marks the presence of a whale – and at their glad cry of "There she blows" the ship instantly springs into life, bustle and activity. With all possible speed, boats are prepared, men hurry to their places, and the boats are lowered away, the mainyard is swung, and the ship is hove-to, and pulled by the long ash oars in the hands of the brawny men, the boat fairly steams through the water toward the great creatures lazily swimming along just ahead.

As the boat approaches closely not a sound is made, not a word uttered by the men, for while his sight is not particularly keen a whale's ears can catch the slightest unusual noise even at a long distance. Stealthily, as if stalking a deer, the boat creeps forward – the men often abandoning the oars and using short paddles – while in the bow, naked to his waist, with hair tossing in the breeze and hands grasping the heavy "iron," stands the boat-steerer, every nerve taut, every sense on the alert and every muscle ready to dart his weapon as soon as the whale is within striking distance. Perchance the great creature "sounds" and his mighty flukes flash for an instant in the air as he dives to the depths, or perhaps some slight noise, some suspicion of danger or a glimpse of his enemies causes him to become "gallied" or frightened. In the former case the boat waits motionless until the whale again reappears, and so practiced have the whalers become that many of them can foresee, merely by the position of the whale's flukes as he sounds, just where and when the whale will rise or "breach" to "blow." If, on the other hand, he is gallied, a long, hard chase commences, the men striving to reach within striking distance and get fast, the whale striving to evade the boat and leading the straining men for weary hours and for mile after mile before the iron at last is fast in the creature's body, or the mate, fearing to lose the ship, orders the chase abandoned. But if all goes well the tiny whaleboat is soon within a score of feet of the huge, black mass that rolls majestically upward – like the bottom of a capsized ship – and which gives no hint of the stupendous power, the awful fury, and the terrible dangers which lurk within.

Closer and closer the boat steals, and with the mate's shout of "Give it to him" the iron is hurled with all the power of the boat-steerer's knotted muscles and the keen steel buries itself in the blubber of the whale. Springing aft, and seizing the great steering oar, the boat-steerer takes the mate's place, while the latter rushes forward to the bow and then commences a battle royal – a fight to the death between the mightiest, most powerful of creatures and six puny men in a cockleshell of a boat.

Stung by the barbed iron in his flesh the whale dashes forward, while the line, attached to the iron, whirrs with a roar through the bow-chock and leaps from the tubs like a living serpent. The stricken creature may sound and seek the unfathomed depths as he strives to rid himself of the smarting iron in his side, or he may rush madly, blindly, forward with the speed of a great steamship. In either case every second is fraught with the greatest danger and most imminent peril of death for the whalemen, and the utmost skill, judgment and rapidity of action are necessary to save themselves and their captive. But they give no heed to the risks, to the menace which confronts them or to their own safety – their one thought is to make a catch, to keep fast until the cetacean is tired out and then to kill him with the lance.

If the whale sounds too far and the last of the line is run out it must be cut to save the boat from being pulled beneath the sea. If the monster dashes straight away the boat may be carried beyond sight of the ship ere the whale can be killed. If he swims rapidly round and round in a circle or "mills" the boat may be capsized, despite every effort of the boat-steerer; or, if this is avoided, it may be impossible to get close enough to use the lance.

And meanwhile there are a thousand lesser dangers to avoid, a score of other matters to attend to, a myriad of details to think of. The whizzing line must be kept clear and must be cooled by throwing water on it. A kink may mean death and destruction. If the line leaps about a man's leg the limb is torn off or the man pulled bodily into the sea. The line must be kept constantly taut by hauling in any slack and coiling it on the bottom of the boat. The mate must watch every opportunity, every chance, to haul close in and kill. The men must obey every order, every gesture, instantly, or lose their lives and the whale, and the boat-steerer with set jaws, gritted teeth and straining muscles must use every ounce of his weight, every atom of his strength and all the skill he possesses to swing the rushing boat, to guide it on its mad course and to prevent it from capsizing as it is towed, hurtling through the sea by the wounded, terrified mountain of flesh and blood to which it is fast. Sometimes two or more boats get fast to one whale, but often the battle is fought entirely by one boat and between shouts of "now haul up," "haul line," "there he mills round," and similar orders, the boat is gradually brought closer and closer to the tired, wounded whale, who by now may have several "irons" in him and may be fast to several boats.

Cautiously the boat creeps forward and each foot, each inch, that the distance from the whale is lessened, the perils of the whalemen increase a hundredfold. If the captive is a right whale a single sweep of the gigantic flukes may smash the boat to atoms and wound, maim or kill men, while if the quarry is a sperm whale there is not only the danger of the ponderous tail, but the far greater peril of the enormous, armed, lower jaw, with its row of gleaming, pointed teeth – a titanic sword wielded by the power of hundreds of tons of muscle.

And there is no way of avoiding flukes or jaw, no avenue of escape left open for the men; their tiny craft is attached to the monster by stout, hempen line, they must approach within the very heart of the danger zone; their lives depend upon the nerves and skill of the mate and a slender lance; their duty is to kill or be killed, and their motto is, "a stove boat or a dead whale."

Dangerous as the landsman might think it to approach a whale and "fasten" with the iron, the perils of "going on and striking" are as nothing compared to making the kill. The smart of the iron, the panic of fright and his efforts to escape cause the whale to seek safety in flight rather than to turn on his enemies when first struck and moreover the boat need not approach closer to the whale than ten or fifteen feet – far too close proximity to suit a landlubber, however.

But it is quite a different matter when using the lance to give the coup-de-grace to the wounded whale. Tired, feeling escape impossible, gallied, nervous, maddened and realizing who and what his assailants are, the monster seeks to destroy them and only waits for them to come within reach ere turning to wreak vengeance with all his fury. Moreover, to kill the whale – by the old-fashioned hand lance – the frail boat must be brought actually alongside the whale, for the lance is not thrown like the iron but is shoved into the whale's vitals by placing the keen point against the creature's side and actually pushing the lance in by main strength. Steady must be the nerves of men to accomplish such a feat, strong their muscles, stout their hearts, great their courage and wonderful their self-reliance, for upon that slender bit of steel, the accuracy of its thrust and the power that drives it, their lives depend.

Even when at last the boat was alongside the whale, when the lance was driven into his body, and the death-blow was given to the monster, the dangers of the men were not ended; in fact the gravest peril of all was yet to come, for rarely did a whale die without a struggle, and in his death throes, or "flurry," many a boat was stove and many a life was lost. Lashing the waves into a maelstrom of churning froth and foam, spouting blood and crimsoning the sea, lifting his mighty flukes and smashing them down with the power of a hundred steam-hammers, rearing his stupendous head and dropping it again to the sea like a descending avalanche and darting, thrusting and sweeping to right and left with his enormous, armed jaw, a sperm whale in his flurry fights furiously to the end and strives to destroy everything within reach ere he breathes his last.

Menaced by the sweeps of his flukes, threatened by the awful jaw, thrown hither and thither by the crimsoned waves created by the writhing giant beside them, the

58

whalemen must strive like madmen to preserve their lives and they only draw calm breaths when at last their victim rolls over on his side, the glad cry of "fin out" rings forth and the chase is over. If there were other whales about and within sight a barbed iron staff bearing a flag and known as a "waif" was planted in the dead whale's side and the tired men resumed the hunt and attacked another monster; perhaps to meet with success, perhaps to have their boat smashed, their bones broken or to find an unmarked watery grave. If, on the other hand, there were no other whales to be taken the crew proceeded to prepare the dead whale for towing to their ship. This consisted in getting a chain around the flukes and while this may sound like easy, simple work compared to capturing and killing the whale, yet it was often difficult and dangerous in the extreme.

Often darkness fell and the sea rose ere the whale was killed, and the boat's crew thus found themselves miles from their ship, a gale blowing, a heavy sea running and inky blackness hiding everything but the combing crests of the waves from view. Beside them, wallowing sluggishly in the sea, just awash, and as dangerous as a reef, lay the carcass of the whale, and to approach the great flukes, to secure a chain to the "small" at the root of the tail and to tow the body to their ship was a Herculean task. Sometimes a light line, with a six- or ten-pound shot attached to its middle, was taken in tow by two boats – when two boats were at hand – and by allowing the weighted line to sink and by dragging the ends towards the whale's head a bight of line was passed under the flukes. To this a heavier rope was bent, and to which a chain was fastened and passed by this means around the tail. But if only one boat was at hand the difficulties were tremendous. Only by actually clinging to the whale was it possible to pass a line around the flukes at times, and held only by a rope around his waist, some daring man would clamber onto the slippery carcass and while half smothered in the waves would succeed in getting a line around the whale's tail and thus enable the crew to secure the fluke-chain and tow their prize to the ship.

At other times, ere darkness fell, or if a storm was seen approaching, the boats would be recalled to the ship by signals and were obliged to leave their hard-earned catch to the mercy of the wind and waves, perchance to find it again, perhaps to lose it forever.

With the ship shorthanded and often miles from the scene of the chase and the kill it was of the utmost importance that a code of signals should be arranged which would deal with any emergency which might arise and that these signals should be thoroughly understood and instantly and implicitly obeyed by those in the boats.

Moreover, from the lofty lookout on the ships' masts, the whales and boats could be seen at far greater distances and much better than from the boats themselves, with their limited horizon, and when rising and falling on the waves, and by means of the prearranged signals the movements of the boats' crews could be directed from the ships. Frequently the distance between boats and ships was too great to permit of regular signal flags being seen or distinguished, and hence most of the signals were given by means of the yards, sails and colors, with the addition of a "masthead waif," a canvas-covered hoop at the end of an eight-foot pole.

In order that there should be no confusion and that each ship should be able to direct its own boats without others in the vicinity knowing the significance of the signals, each whaling ship had its private code, but as all were more or less alike the following will serve as a very good example of all:

Whales up: Color up at foremast
Whales between ship and boat: Colors at half-mast
Whales ahead of ship: Flying jib, or jib, down
Whales further ahead: Flying jib, or jib, up and down

Whales two points off weather bow: Fore topgallant sail on the cap

Whales four points on weather bow: Weather clew of fore topgallant sail on the cap

Whales four points on leebow: Lee clew of fore topgallant sail on the cap

Whales on weather bow: Main topgallant sail on the cap

Whales on lee bow: Haul up lee clew of main topgallant sail

Whales right astern: Spanker up

Boat fast: Signals at fore and main masts

Stove boat: Two signals at the main mast

One boat come aboard: Two signals at mizzen peak

Come aboard (all boats): One signal at mizzen peak

Boats hove up: Colors up at fore

When the topgallant sails are not set the courses (lower sails) will be used in their place. Thus by watching the signals set on their ship the boats' crews could locate whales which they could not see; they knew if an accident had happened to their companions and could go to their rescue; they knew if their presence was required on board, and they felt that at all times they were under the watchful eye of their captain and could place implicit faith in the signals that he set for their guidance.

6 - TRUE STORIES OF WHALING

IN ADDITION TO THE PERILS of the sea to which merchant sailors are exposed, the whalemen faced innumerable dangers absolutely unknown to other seamen, and yet the losses among whaling vessels and their crews were no greater than in other professions of the sea. Moreover, comparatively few of the whalers' losses were due to causes which destroy merchant vessels and their men and the very dangers which merchant sailors dread the most played a very small part in the casualties of the whalemen.

Fire, collisions at sea, wrecks on rocks or reefs and vessels foundering in storms are the commonest of ocean tragedies in the merchant marine, even though the vessels sail on regular routes and through familiar seas and are hedged about with every care and precaution for their safety. But among whalemen such perils were of little moment and were quite lost to sight amid the greater dangers peculiar to their calling.

Fire was very rare, although the grease-soaked planks and timbers of the ships were highly inflammable; the vessels weathered the heaviest seas and strongest gales of the stormiest and most tempestuous parts of the oceans for years at a time and seldom did the whalers touch bottom, even when cruising on unknown seas bristling with uncharted reefs and rocks. Terrific indeed was the storm which alone could injure a whaleship, and when a whaling vessel did take the ground her huge timbers and thick planking usually protected her from serious injury. Many a whaleship left her bones to bleach upon reefs, rocks or islands thousands of miles from home; many foundered in mid-ocean; many were destroyed by fire and many met a fate unknown; but when we consider the many hundred vessels that were devoted to whaling through more than two centuries, the length of time they were at sea, the risks they ran, and the out-of-the-world places they visited the total losses were marvelously small.

Many of the ships went forth time after time on cruises of several years' duration; sailed to the uttermost parts of the world, braved the elements of the frigid and the tropic zones on every sea, held their own most creditably through several generations of skippers, and are still strong, staunch and seaworthy today. Many an old whaleman sailed forth from New Bedford or some other port in the same ship throughout his long life and never had a mishap and never lost a man on all his voyages.

One Nantucket captain, over eighty years of age, boasted that in all the years he had been whaling – he commenced as a boy – his ship had never touched bottom, that not a man had ever been lost or abandoned from his vessel, that no man had ever been off duty over a week on account of illness or injuries, that he had never lost but one spar, that he had never returned without a full cargo of oil, and that he had never passed a day at sea without going aloft himself, save in the heaviest gales. This man was not exceptional; there were scores, yes hundreds, who could say as much, for the Yankee whaling captains were unequaled seamen, born navigators, and never shirked their duty; but through fair weather or foul, through calm and storm, amid vast ice-floes or roaring breakers, followed their quarry round the world and back with consummate skill and wondrous courage.

Of all dangers which beset the whalemen perhaps the least expected was that of a whale ramming the ship itself and yet this happened many times and many a ship was sent to the bottom by a maddened whale smashing in her planks with the tremendous force of his massive bulk and enormous strength.

Among the numerous records of such catastrophes is the case of the Nantucket ship *Essex*, in charge of Captain George Pollard, Jr. No doubt other ships had met the same fate previously, but no records are available, and the

Essex is probably the first-known instance of a ship sunk by being rammed by a whale, as well as one of the most awful of ocean tragedies of which we have authentic details.[17]

On August 12, 1819, the *Essex* sailed from Nantucket for the Pacific grounds and after a fair passage and no unusual events rounded Cape Horn and bore northward, cruising for sperm whales, until November 29, when the call of "There she blows" rang from the lookout, the ship was hove-to, and the boats were lowered. The chief mate's boat was soon fast, but no sooner did the whale feel the "iron" than with a stroke of his flukes he stove the boat and the men were obliged to cut loose. Stripping off their jackets they stuffed the garments into the gaping holes in the planking and by means of this makeshift and by constant bailing managed to reach their ship in safety. Meanwhile the captain's and second mate's boats were fast to a whale and the chief mate swung the yards and headed the ship toward them.

The men were busily at work, repairing their stove boat, and the mate was in charge of the quarter-deck when a whale of about eighty-five feet in length breached from the water less than twenty rods distant. Without an instant's hesitation the monster headed for the *Essex* at full speed and with a terrific crash struck her just forward of the fore chains. For a few moments the creature lay as if stunned, and then recovering, started away to leeward. As the ship was leaking rapidly the pumps were at once started and signals were set recalling the absent boats to the ship. Suddenly the whale reappeared, rested for a few moments thrashing the sea with his flukes and opening and closing his gigantic jaws, and then gathering all his strength, once more dashed full into the vessel, staving in her heavy planks close to the catheads.

---

[17] It remains probably the most famous real life whaling disaster. It was the inspiration for *Moby Dick* and was made into a movie (*In The Heart Of The Sea*) in 2015.

Within two minutes the ship was on her beam-ends and seeing that it was hopeless to try to save her the injured boat was gotten over and the mate and the men on board hastily tumbled into her. Captain Pollard now reached the scene and ordered the masts cut away so that the vessel would right. This was done, the decks were scuttled in order to reach supplies and for three days the boats stood by their ship, repairing and building up their frail whaleboats, one of which had been stove. At the end of the third day the seas had greatly enlarged the holes made by the infuriated whale and the *Essex* was seen to be going to pieces very rapidly. There was nothing to be gained by waiting longer and in the three tiny boats the men headed for the coast of Peru, nearly 3,000 miles away.

This was on the twenty-third of November and day after day the men toiled at the oars; scorched by a tropic sun, parched with thirst, and faint with hunger, for the provisions and water they had been able to secure from the ship were scarce enough to preserve life.

Five days after deserting the *Essex*, barren Ducie's Island was reached and the crews landed. Aside from a few shellfish and seabirds there was nothing to eat upon the place and no water could be obtained, and on December 27 they again set forth, after leaving three men who refused to go farther, and who preferred to die upon this wave-washed islet, rather than endure the tortures of hunger and thirst in the open boats. Great as had been their privations before reaching the island they were as nothing compared to the torments the men underwent on that long, terrible row of 2,500 miles to Juan Fernandez. On January 10, 1820, the second mate died and two days later the boats became separated. One by one the members of the crew succumbed to their thirst, hunger and exposure, and as they died their companions fell upon their bodies, cut them to pieces and devoured the raw flesh like famished wolves. Two of the boats, those of the captain and the second mate, remained together until

January 29, by which time four men had died and had been devoured and the survivors once more faced death by starvation, when the captain suggested they should draw lots to see who would be killed to save the others.

But deliverance was now close at hand, and on February 17 the chief mate's boat was sighted by the British brig *Indian* and the three survivors were taken aboard. Five days later the ship *Dauphin* of Nantucket sighted a weather-beaten, tossing whaleboat, and bearing down upon her found Captain Pollard and Charles Ramsdale still alive, the sole survivors of their boat's crew.

The third boat was never heard from and the story of her occupants was never known, but those who were saved ultimately recovered and Captain Pollard, in later years, was employed as a deck-hand on Fulton's famous steamboat, the *Hudson.*

Somewhat similar but with a far happier ending was the case of the *Ann Alexander* of New Bedford; Captain John S. Deblois, which sailed on a whaling cruise on January 1, 1858. On August 20, the mate's boat was fast to a whale when the creature suddenly turned, seized the boat in his jaws and smashed it to bits. The captain at once hurried to the assistance of the struggling men, took them into his boat and headed for the ship.

Meanwhile the boat had been lowered and sent to assist the captain with his over-crowded boat, the crews were divided between the two boats, and once more the indomitable whalers attacked the whale, but again the monster turned and in an instant stove the second boat. The captain's boat was now loaded to the water's edge with eighteen men and as it was useless to attempt to capture the whale under these conditions the boat was again headed towards the ship, now six or seven-miles distant. Hardly had they started when the whale gave chase with open jaws and the men felt their last hour had come; but for some reason the creature veered off, passed the boat within a few feet and disappeared, leaving the boat to reach the *Alexander* unharmed.

As soon as the men were on board, the boat was sent back to pick up the oars and fittings of the other boats and the whale again appearing, the chase was resumed, but when within fifty rods of the creature, he sounded, and the attempt at capture was abandoned and the boat was pulled slowly towards the approaching ship. The captain was standing at the vessel's knightheads watching the boat draw near when suddenly the whale rose close at hand and before an order could be shouted dashed into the ship, staving a huge hole two feet from the keel and just abaft the foremast. Into the torn and started planking the sea rushed in a torrent and the men had barely time to toss a few provisions into a boat and launch it, ere the ship plunged beneath the waves.

The predicament of the men, thus suddenly left afloat in mid-ocean, was a serious one indeed, for one of the boats had been badly stove and leaked rapidly and less than one day's stock of water and food was on hand for all the men. Undismayed, however, the crews started to pull across the sea toward land, but two days later, on August 22, their troubles came to an end as the ship *Nantucket* of Nantucket was sighted.

Strangely enough the whale which attacked and sunk the *Alexander* was afterwards captured by a New Bedford whaling ship, the *Rebecca Simms*. Five months after the foundering of the *Ann Alexander* a whale was killed by the *Simms* and pieces of ship's timbers and planks were noticed embedded in his head and an examination revealed two of the *Alexander's* irons in his body.

Still another whaling ship which was deliberately rammed and sunk by a whale was the bark *Kathleen* of New Bedford. This, moreover, is one of the most recent, if not the latest instance of its sort, for it occurred in 1901, when the Kathleen was cruising in the Atlantic to the east of the Leeward Islands in the West Indies.

A whale had been struck but the iron drew and the wounded creature turned and hurled itself at the bark. The blow tore away several feet of planking, smashed the timbers, and the vessel filled so rapidly that the crew, as well as the captain's wife, who was on board, were obliged to take to the boats immediately.

Fortunately for them land was not far-distant, and although the boats separated all arrived safely without the loss of a life, one boat reaching Dominica, another Barbados and a third being picked up by a passing ship. Had their vessel been sunk in mid-ocean their fate might have been far more terrible than that of the survivors of the *Essex*.

Many another similar case is to be found in the logbooks, journals and records of whalers, but these will serve as examples.

Still a stranger fate, which befell several whalers and merchant ships as well, was running onto whales – the result being the same as if they had struck a rock or a reef – and while some were actually sunk in this manner the majority of the vessels which ran onto whales were brought into port, though leaking badly. The earliest record of a vessel thus ramming a whale was in 1640, when a ship ran upon a whale during a gale and struck with such force as to put the ship "in stays" besides staving in the planks, six timbers and a beam, as well as broaching two hogsheads of vinegar which were in the forehold.

In March, 1796, the ship *Harmony* of Rochester, Captain George Blankenship, ran on a whale when off the coast of Brazil and was sunk, but while the ship and cargo were lost the crew escaped in the boats. In 1859 the ship *Herald* of the *Morning* arrived at Hampton Roads leaking badly and reported striking a whale when off Cape Horn. The force of the blow had started seven feet of her stem as far as the wood-ends and the bobstay had been carried away. That the whale suffered even more as a result of the collision was proven by the fact that it was seen to "spout blood" as it swam away – a sure sign of a fatal injury.

A year later, in 1860, the steamer *Eastern City* ran into a whale while en route to St. John, and although this creature was a mere infant fifty feet in length, the impact displaced the steamer's cutwater. Again in 1865 the British schooner *Forest Oak*, bound from Boston to Yarmouth, Nova Scotia, struck a whale with such force as to loosen the foremast and throw all the men off their feet. Then in 1873 the three-masted schooner, *Watanga* of Wilmington, North Carolina, while running at a speed of six or seven knots, struck a whale and tore off the false stem, split the stem, and started the planks. The bobstay parted, the bowsprit went adrift and it was with the greatest difficulty that the vessel was kept afloat until reaching port.

There are many other instances of a similar sort and the terrific impact of a ship thus striking a motionless whale may be appreciated by the report of the captain of the merchant ship *Cuban*, of Greenock, which ran onto a sleeping whale while sailing to Demerara in 1857. Although this was a five-hundred-ton ship under full sail and was deeply laden, her headway was stopped and she was brought to a standstill as suddenly and completely as if she had been run upon the solid shore.

But of all shipwrecks caused by running onto a whale, that of the ship *Union*, of Nantucket, captain Edward Gardner, is the most noteworthy and interesting.

The *Union* sailed from Nantucket for Brazil on September 19, 1807, and when twelve days out and while proceeding under easy sail at a speed of seven knots she suddenly brought up against a whale. The shock was so great that those on board thought the vessel had run onto a rock until the animal was seen and a hasty examination showed that the planking on the starboard bow had been smashed in and two timbers had been broken. The pump was started but the water rapidly gained and the crew prepared to leave the ship.

The accident occurred at ten o'clock at 'night – it was no doubt owing to the darkness that the whale was not sighted – and by midnight the boats were lowered and pulled away from the sinking vessel. A heavy sea was running, and the crew of sixteen men were scattered among three boats. Fearing that the boats might become separated in the darkness and in order to give more shifts at the oars one boat was abandoned and the men were divided equally in the two remaining boats, which then headed for the Azores, over 600 miles distant.

By October 2 the men managed to rig up sails, but during the next two days the wind rose to a gale, the extemporized sails were carried away and the two boats were lashed together and allowed to drift. Owing to the haste in which the men left the ship very few provisions and an insufficient supply of water had been put in the boats, and by October 4 the men were put on rations consisting of but three quarts of water and sixteen small cakes for the whole company for each twenty-four hours.

Starvation was staring them in the face, their thirst was terrible, and their case seemed hopeless, when on October 9, they sighted the island of Flores and landed safely after being adrift for seven days and eight nights, during which time they had rowed, sailed and drifted for six hundred miles. I have mentioned the irons of the *Alexander* being found in the whale which sank that ship, and which was later taken by the *Rebecca Simms*, and while this may seem like a most remarkable coincidence, a mere chance, and in a work of fiction would appear highly improbable, yet such cases were of common occurrence.

Among the thousands of whales taken by the hundreds of whaling vessels, which scoured the oceans in the heyday of the industry, it would have been strange indeed if now and then irons were not found in the whales captured. Countless irons were lost by the whales escaping, the boats being obliged to cut loose or the whale destroying the boats and going off with all their gear sticking in his side. As all the irons were marked, the ships to which they belonged were easily identified, and if irons belonging to a ship which had met with disaster or unusual adventures were found, the fact was reported, but otherwise a line in a logbook was the only record of irons found in whales.

At times some whale would be killed bearing irons which told of a lapse of years since he was first struck, and which threw light upon the movements of whales or upon channels unknown to man. Thus in 1815, Captain Peter Paddok of the *Lady Adams* killed a whale which contained an iron thrown by the same captain when in command of the ship *Lion* thirteen years before and in a far-distant part of the Pacific.

So, too, irons used in Davis' Straits were found on several occasions in whales captured in the Arctic and this proved to whalers as well as to geographers and explorers that an open Northwest Passage really existed. Sometimes stories of a "mad whale" were spread among the whalers – tales of some monster of exceptional ferocity and courage – a whale warrior who destroyed lives and boats and invariably escaped, and when at last some vessel captured such a fighter and identified him by the irons found in his body the report was circulated among all the whalers far and near. Such an incident was reported by the ship *Hector* of New Bedford. In October 1832, the boats were lowered and started after a large whale, but before they were within striking distance the creature turned, stove one of the boats and threw its occupants into the sea. The captain's boat hurried to their rescue, but the furious, fighting whale dashed at it, seized it in his enormous, armed jaw and chewed and smashed it to pieces. The mate, struggling in the water, was then seized by the creature and although bitten and chewed and badly wounded he was finally released alive. Meanwhile the other boats had drawn near and fearlessly attacked the whale, and despite his ferocity and resistance the men succeeded in killing him.

When he was cut up irons of the ship *Barclay* were found buried in him and he was thus identified as being a well-known fighter which had already destroyed several boats and men, among them the first mate of the *Barclay*, who had been killed three months previously. The danger of being seized and bitten by a whale was only one of the many perils of the chase and numerous instances of men killed and injured in this manner are recorded, while stories of stove boats, men wounded by the thrashing flukes, and tales of hairbreadth escapes are innumerable.

It was an everyday occurrence to have boats stove and the men thrown into the sea by a wounded or "fast" whale, and the crews took this as a matter of course, but several such incidents are well worthy of mention. The first instance of the sort recorded was in 1766, when a sperm whale rammed a boat, threw out the son of the captain and catching the unfortunate man carried him off in his jaws. More remarkable was the case of Marshall Jenkins, who in 1870 attacked and struck a sperm whale. The wounded creature turned on the boat, bit it in two, seized Jenkins in his jaws and sounded. The rest of the crew clung to the two pieces of the boat, which still floated, and were waiting for a boat from the ship to come to their rescue when the whale breached from the water close at hand and, to the wonder of the men, threw the mate into the forepart of the broken boat.

Marvelous as it may seem Jenkins was still alive and although "much bruised," as the log relates, he recovered within a fortnight and was none the worse for his strange adventure – an escape so miraculous that it probably has no equal.

Almost as remarkable was the case of a whaling captain who was thrown into the water from a boat stove by a right whale. The whale turned on the swimmer who dove under the creature's body and for three-quarters of an hour the struggle between man and whale continued, the boats being unable to approach close enough to rescue their comrade or to strike the whale.

Diving, swimming and dodging, the captain strove to evade the huge creature while the whale struck at him with its flukes, or rearing its stupendous head in the air, brought it crashing down upon the half-drowned man. Fortunately for the whaleman he succeeded in avoiding a direct blow and while buffeted and bruised by the whale's flukes and dashed far beneath the waves by the descending head he escaped serious injury. Knowing that the tip of a right, whale's nose is extremely sensitive and that the slightest injury to this portion of his head will turn a whale, the captain drew his sheath knife and endeavored to drive it into his assailant's nose. At last, he was successful and, the whale retreating, the captain was dragged into the boat more dead than alive, thoroughly exhausted, but with comparatively slight injuries from his terrific battle with the monster.

Sometimes, however, the whales proved the salvation of the men they attempted to destroy. Such was the case when the boats of Captain Huntling struck a bull sperm whale off the Rio de la Plata. This whale seized the boat in his jaws and chewed it to bits, but another boat rescued the men, while two others went on and planted irons in the whale. Again, the creature turned on his enemies, crushed the boats with his jaw, and left twelve men struggling in the sea. Several were scarcely able to swim, and to save themselves two of them actually clambered upon the whale's back and perched astride his hump while a third clung to his side until all were rescued by another boat.

The whale now had six irons in his body and was fast to three lines of three hundred fathoms each, but despite this he was still full of fight and succeeded in smashing another boat. The captain then fired a bomb, loaded with six ounces of powder, into the creature, but instead of killing him it seemed merely to madden him the more and before the boats could escape the whale dashed among them, tossing them to the right and left, and then disappeared, carrying with him twelve hundred fathoms of line and all the gear and leaving the disappointed whalemen with nothing but four broken boats to show for their long and futile battle. It is rather remarkable that more serious injuries did not result from the staving-in of boats by the whales, for the keen irons and lances, hatchets, fluke-spades, oars and even the lines all threatened life and limb when thrown helter-skelter among the struggling men. If a whale was fast when a boat was stove or capsized, the whizzing, rushing line was liable to drag men under the waves or even tear them to pieces, and several instances are recorded of men being terribly injured by being caught in a turn of a line attached to a wounded whale.

One such case occurred when the boats of the Provincetown bark, *Parker Cook*, attacked a whale in 1850. Two boats were lowered and the mate's boat-steerer succeeded in putting two irons into the whale. The creature sounded, breached under the boat and capsized it and a kink of the line caught around the boat-steerer's leg. The whale then turned to attack the captain's boat, which had approached and attempted to seize it in his jaw but was killed by a bomb lance in the hands of the skipper. The boat-steerer's leg was nearly severed from his body and he died from his injuries later. Even after the whales were killed the whalers' perils were not over and many boats' crews were lost by being towed beyond sight of their ship by a whale and finding it impossible to regain their vessel after their captive was killed. Numerous boats' crews thus parted from their vessels were picked up by other whaleships nearby; others were never heard from, and no doubt died a lingering and awful death by thirst, starvation and exposure, while still others managed to survive the most fearful privations and ultimately landed on the nearest coast. But among them all probably none had a more marvelous story or a more miraculous escape than the men of the bark *Janet* of Westport.

On the twenty-third of January 1849, the *Janet's* men struck and killed a whale late in the afternoon and while towing their prize towards the ship the boat was capsized, and although the men succeeded in righting their craft the boat's keg of water, buckets, compass, lantern, paddles and other contents were lost. A heavy sea was running and to prevent the water-filled boat from foundering oars were lashed across her. Night was now approaching, the seas were constantly breaking over the boat and the crew tried frantically to make their plight known to their comrades on the distant ship. Finding this unsuccessful and realizing that no aid was coming to them, the men worked their boat to the side of the dead whale and endeavored to empty the water from it, but the sea was too heavy and abandoning the attempt the men cut loose from the whale and started to work their all but submerged craft towards the vessel whose lights were now visible.

All night long they labored through the huge seas and against the gale, but by morning found they were steadily losing ground and had not been sighted by those on the bark. Unable to make headway the boat was put about before the wind and allowed to drift while the men, giving up all hope, but still undaunted, strove to rest and recover their exhausted strength.

On the second morning the wind died down, and as the waves grew less the crew attempted to throw over their boat and empty some of the water from her. In this they were successful, but one man was lost while doing it and the sufferings of the others, – who had been up to their arms in water for forty-eight hours and without a morsel of food or a drop of water in all that time – were so great that two of the men went mad. That all were not crazed is remarkable, for the nearest land was Cocos Island, off the Peruvian coast, one thousand miles distant and not one of the men was able to pull an oar. By dint of the utmost exertion and Herculean efforts the ceiling was torn from the boat and made into a rough, wooden sail and propelled by this sad makeshift the starving, thirst-mad men floated across the trackless ocean.

With no compass to guide them, steering a course by the stars, they sailed onward over a brassy sea and under a scorching tropic sun. No shower brought relief or the blessed water they craved so much, not a crumb of food or a drop to drink passed their lips for seven days, and then, driven to extremities, lots were drawn and one of the men was butchered and eaten. Hardly had this been done when a shower fell, but it came too late, and on the eighth day another man died from suffering and exposure. On the ninth day another shower furnished them with water, and, as if sent by Providence, a dolphin actually leaped into the boat. This served to save their lives, and for several days thereafter birds approached so closely that the men were able to kill them, and thus provided for, as by a miracle, the men reached Cocos Island on July 13, twenty days after being capsized. Landing upon the island the men soon managed to kill a wild pig and two days later were rescued by the *Leonidas* of New Bedford.

Great as were their sufferings in their open whaleboats the crews often refused to be picked up and after securing water and provisions held their course in their own boat. One boat's crew was adrift for nine days when it was spoken by a Norwegian bark, but the men refused to go aboard as she was headed for England. The following day the ocean waifs were picked up by a whaling vessel, and so dazed were the men by exposure and privation that two weeks elapsed before they realized they were not aboard their own vessel.

Several instances are also recorded in which whalemen have actually sailed for tremendous distances to their home ports and two boats lost from the schooner *John R. Manta* in 1915, when off Hatteras, succeeded in making New Bedford in safety. Fire, as already mentioned, was rare on whaling ships and few vessels were destroyed in this manner. A notable instance is that of the *Cassander* of Providence; not only on account of the privations of her crew but because of the inconceivable inhumanity of the merchant captain who refused to rescue them.

The *Cassander*, under Captain Henry Winslow, sailed from Providence on the nineteenth of November 1847, and on the first of May, 1848, fire was discovered in the lower hold near the foremast, where four barrels of tar were stored. As soon as the cry of "fire" was raised two members of the crew – negroes from Africa – leaped overboard, and although a rope was thrown to them they refused to take it and one soon sank. The second mate's boat was then lowered and rescued the other negro, who subsequently confessed that he and his companion had set fire to the ship for fear of being made slaves and that his comrade had shot himself before jumping into the sea. As a half gale was blowing from the northwest the fire gained rapidly and finding that it was impossible to save the ship three boats were lowered and the crew of twenty-three men managed to get away in safety. Owing to the location of the fire and its rapid spread it was impossible to reach the supply of water and provisions on board and the men were put on a ration of one gill of water and half a biscuit per day. The wind blew with such force that sails could not be used and the men were obliged to row constantly through the enormous seas kicked up by the gale.

As the sea grew calmer and the men became exhausted fragments of sails were set, and on the fifth of May a vessel was sighted. She proved to be a Spanish brig bound from Barcelona for Montevideo, and as the shipwrecked men drew alongside the captain ordered them away. Despite their pleas and entreaties this inhuman creature refused even to take the boats in tow or to allow their crews a night's rest on board and finally, disheartened, disappointed, and raving at his brutality the boats' crews gave up in despair. Unable to row against the gale, which now arose, the men lashed oars together and threw them over as a sea-anchor and all through the next twenty-four hours rode the billows to this drag. At four in the afternoon of the seventh of May a heavy sea buried the captain's boat and swamped her, and although the men were rescued by the other boats all their precious store of water and their instruments were lost.

The following morning the wind fell and a heavy shower brought relief from thirst, and with renewed strength and fresh courage the men bent again to the oars, and on the tenth day of May reached the coast of Brazil. Wrecks through stress of weather were unusual among the whalers, but several cases are recorded of vessels going to the bottom by having their planks eaten to pieces by teredos, or shipworms,[18] as for example, the ship *Niphon* of Nantucket which foundered at sea on January 12, 1849, while returning home from her first voyage.

Most of the vessels which foundered, however, ran on uncharted reefs, as was the case with the *Canton* of New Bedford, which on the fourth of March 1854, struck a reef in the Pacific. With only half a pint of water and half a biscuit per day for each man the crew set forth in four boats in a gale of wind and a heavy sea. Owing to the rough weather they were unable to reach the nearest islands and after forty-five days landed on one of the uninhabited islands of the Ladrones. Here they succeeded in capturing a few birds and fish and then again set forth for Tinian, thirty miles distant, where they were mistaken for pirates. After some parley they proved their identity and were allowed to land and obtain provisions, and then, once more embarking in the tiny boats which had served them so well, they headed for Guam, which they reached four days later, after a voyage of more than four thousand miles.

It was indeed fortunate for the men of the *Canton* that they reached islands where the natives were friendly, for

---

[18] Marine bivalve mollusks from the family of saltwater clams.

in many of the South Sea islands they would have met a worse fate than drowning or dying of exposure. Many of the islands were inhabited by cannibals and in some of the others the natives had been so brutally treated by whalers that they were ready to wreak summary vengeance upon any defenseless white men whom they met. Not infrequently the ships themselves were attacked when they put into some of the South Sea islands for supplies, and while the superior arms of the whalemen usually drove off the savages with great losses, yet now and again the natives were successful, and the whalemen were butchered and their ships destroyed.

On October 5, 1835, the ship *Awashonks* of Falmouth hove-to off Namarik Island (one of the Marshall Group) to recruit natives, her crew and officers little dreaming of the tragedy to be enacted on their decks. About noon a number of the islanders came on board and the captain and first and second mates went below for dinner, leaving the third mate in charge of the deck. As soon as his superiors had finished their meal, Mr. Jones, the third officer, went below, returning in about fifteen minutes to join the others on deck. Three men were aloft working at the rigging, one man was on watch below, and others were forward, while still another was at the helm.

Suddenly, and without the least warning, the crowd of natives rushed for the whale-spades, seized the keen-edged instruments, and with wild yells dashed at the surprised white men. A blow with a spade killed the helmsman, another spade in the hands of a savage beheaded the captain, and the first mate was butchered as he leaped down the forehatch.

The second mate strove to reach safety by running out on the bowsprit, but was caught and clubbed to death, while the third mate seized a spade and hurled it at a native who was attacking him. The savage dodged the spade, which buried itself harmlessly in the woodwork, and the officer, now the only white man left alive on deck, ran for his life and leaped down the forehatch where the remaining members of the crew had taken refuge.

Fearing to go below to attack the men, the natives shut and fastened down the hatches, thus imprisoning the crew, and then headed the vessel for the shore, intending to wreck her. Meanwhile the three men aloft had escaped the attack of the natives, and now descending as far as they dared they slashed through the braces, allowing the yards to swing to and the ship, thus out of control, drifted towards the open sea.

Below, the third mate and crew were also busy, for they had determined upon a most dangerous expedient. Working their way aft they secured muskets in the cabin, and while the men kept the natives at bay by firing through the skylights the third officer brought a keg of powder, emptied a quantity of its contents on the upper step of the companionway and laid a train of powder down the steps to the cabin.

The train was then fired and the explosion which followed wounded and killed several of the savages, while the others, terrified, were easily driven overboard by the men who rushed up the companionway to the deck. Sometimes the whalemen turned the tables on their assailants and succeeded in accomplishing feats worthy of a dime-novel hero. They were resourceful men, accustomed to taking enormous risks and fighting against great odds and never hesitated to undertake seemingly impossible tasks. To relate all the incidents of their bravery and prowess would require a volume, but no story of whaling would be complete without an account of how two Nantucket captains outwitted a gang of pirates and made their capture easy.

It was in April 1771, that two Nantucket sloops, under command of Isaiah Chadwick and Obed Barker, were lying quietly at anchor in the harbor of Abaco Island in the Bahamas, when a ship was seen in the offing flying signals for assistance.

With the whaleman's readiness to help his fellows, one of the captains lowered a boat and with his men pulled to the strange vessel and went aboard. Hardly had he reached the deck when a pistol was placed at his head and he was ordered to pilot the ship to the inner harbor or have his brains blown out. To this he replied that he would gladly take the ship in, but that he was himself a stranger and unfamiliar with the channel but that one of his men knew the way. The man he designated was then called on board and was threatened like his captain, and as resistance was useless he piloted the vessel into the harbor, but craftily brought her to anchor where a point of land lay between her and the two whaling vessels.

The whalemen were then allowed to go to their own vessel and the two Nantucket captains at once held a council as to the best means of capturing the strangers whom they were convinced were pirates, for while on the strange ship the captain and his man had noticed that the crew was heavily armed and that an unarmed man sat alone in a cabin under guard. From this they judged that the ship had been captured by pirates or by mutineers and that the lone captive was the real commander. After some consultation an invitation was sent to the captain of the pirates, asking him to dine on the sloop, and this was accepted and the captain with his boatswain came aboard the whaler, bringing the captive commander with them for safety. No sooner were they on board than hidden whalemen sprang forth and seized and bound the visitors, and it was then learned that the vessel hailed from Bristol, Rhode Island.

The former commander told his rescuers that he had sailed from Bristol for the coast of Africa, had obtained a cargo of slaves, had carried them to the West Indies and had set sail for home when his crew mutinied and seized the ship with the intention of turning pirates. As none of the men could navigate he and, the mate had been spared, but had been kept under guard and compelled to obey his former crew. After hearing the story the whaling captains told the pirate boatswain that if he would go aboard his ship, release the former mate, who was held a prisoner below decks, and would aid in retaking the ship, they would try to clear him of his part in the mutiny. They then added that they knew a man-o'-war was within two hours' sail and that if the boatswain did not fulfill his promises they would sail to the war vessel, secure an armed force and return and capture all the pirates.

The boatswain was then sent to his ship, and as the whalemen had foreseen, he made no attempt to carry out their orders and one of the Nantucket vessels then hoisted sail and started as if to pass close to one side of the pirates. Immediately the mutineers shifted all their guns to that side of their vessel, but as soon as the whalers saw this had been done they suddenly veered, jibed, and swept by the ship on the opposite side and out of range before the pirates could shift their cannons.

The whalers then sailed out of sight, tacked, set a signal as if they had spoken the man-o'-war and steered boldly in towards the pirate ship. Fully believing that the whalers had carried out their threat and had obtained an armed force of bluejackets, the pirates hastily abandoned their vessel and sought refuge on the shore, only to be quickly captured by the inhabitants. The whalemen then released the captive mate and put a crew aboard the ship and convoyed her to Nassau where the leader of the mutineers was hung and the resourceful whalemen were given a reward of $2,500 for their part in the capture of the pirates.

The whalemen at times had mutinies of their own which were far more serious than this, however, and while many were nipped in the bud, or were suppressed before the mutineers were successful, on several occasions the officers were butchered, and the ships seized by the crews. Among the noteworthy mutinies on whaling ships was that of the *Globe* of Nantucket which occurred in 1824, and which scarcely has a parallel for the petty events which caused it.

The *Globe* sailed from Nantucket in December 1822, and no signs of dissatisfaction or trouble with the crew occurred for over a year. While skylarking on deck one day one of the boat-steerers, named Comstock, was thrown in a wrestling match with the third mate, Noah Fisher, and, infuriated at the latter's triumph, he became so insolent and aggressive that he was knocked down, and slunk out of sight, muttering threats to kill the officer.

No attention was given to his threats, however, and nothing more was thought of the matter until on the night of January 25, 1824, the awful tragedy occurred, when Comstock with four companions entered the cabin and killed the captain and first mate while they slept. Aroused by the noise the second and third mates, Lambert and Fisher, barricaded themselves in their cabin but Comstock loaded two muskets and shot through the door, one of the balls striking Fisher in the mouth. The door was then battered in and Comstock struck at Lambert, but missing him lost his balance and fell into the stateroom where he was seized by the mate, but after a short struggle escaped.

Fisher, armed with a bayonet, lunged at Comstock but the latter promised to spare the men if they would surrender, and Fisher, suffering terribly and badly wounded by the musket ball, threw down his arms, whereupon his brains were promptly blown out and Lambert's body was run through by a whale-lance. With fiendish ferocity the mutineers then mutilated their victims and tossed them overboard, although Lambert was still alive and screaming for mercy.

The vessel was now in the mutineers' hands and was headed for the Mulgrave Islands, where the mutineers proceeded to strip and loot her. Very soon, however, a drunken quarrel arose over the division of the spoils, and during the fight Comstock, the ringleader, was killed. Taking advantage of the confusion, six of the men who had refused to join the mutineers cut the ship's cable, worked the vessel out of the bay and headed out to sea.

After a long and stormy voyage the six men managed to reach Valparaiso, where they turned the ship over to the American consul and related the circumstances of the mutiny and their escape. The ship was then put in charge of a Captain King and sent home, while a vessel was dispatched to the island to capture the mutineers. Upon arrival there it was found that the murderers had already met with their deserts and that all but two men, William Lay of New London and Cyrus Hussey of New Bedford, had been killed by the natives.

Another notable mutiny on a whaling ship took place on the ship *Junior* of New Bedford in 1857. The *Junior* sailed from New Bedford in July, rounded Cape Horn and cruised on the Pacific until December. On Christmas day Captain Miller served spirits to the men and leaving them apparently happy and enjoying their celebration of the day, he retired to his cabin, never again to arise.

Early the following morning, December 26, Cyrus Plummer and four men armed with guns entered the cabin, placed the muzzles of their weapons against the bodies of the sleeping officers and fired. The captain was killed instantly and the mates were riddled by bullets, but still lived. The third mate was quickly dispatched by a whale-spade as he attempted to rise, but the second and first mates managed to escape, and concealed themselves in the hold, although the latter had six bullets in his body.

Having accomplished their purpose in the cabin, the murderers regained the deck, only to be met by the members of the crew who still remained loyal, but after a short parley all gave in to the mutineers. Now that the ship was in their hands the crew devoted themselves to making merry for several days, but soon realized that they were helpless upon the ocean with no one to navigate their vessel. Their first fury had now worn off and the two mates were called from the hold, where they had remained for five days suffering excruciating tortures from their un-cared-for wounds. As their services were required by the mutineers their lives were spared and they were ordered to sail the vessel to Australia. When within twenty miles of the coast, the ringleader, Plummer, ordered two boats lowered and after rifling the ship of valuables and provisions left the vessel and pulled for the land.

Their freedom was short-lived, however; eight of them were caught and hung, and before their execution made a written confession of the part they had played in the tragedy, exonerating the other members of the ship's company, and by thus turning State's evidence the ringleader, Plummer, managed to escape the gallows – which was certainly a great pity. It seems impossible that anything as serious as a mutiny could be humorous, but one mutiny occurred on a whaler which possessed all the elements of a comedy, and as it did not result seriously for any of those concerned it was really amusing. About six years ago the schooner Pedro Varela of New Bedford sailed on a whaling cruise with an "all-American" crew – otherwise miscellaneous riff-raff from slums and gutters-bound for the Atlantic.

By the end of the first season the men were heartily sick and tired of whaling and pined for the easy life of the streets and park benches of the New England cities. Far too cowardly to mutiny and repeat the tragedy of the Junior, these "bums" hit upon a most novel plan of compelling the vessel to return to port, a scheme which proved far more efficacious than open rebellion. During the dark hours of the night watches, the handspikes for the windlass, the blubber tackles and hooks, the carpenter's tools, the wrenches, the irons, the lances, and in fact every tool, implement and weapon used in capturing, cutting or boiling whales, were dropped silently into the sea. So completely did the men carry out their plan to make further whaling impossible that even the grindstone was disposed of and the captain and officers suddenly discovered that no matter how many whales were sighted the creatures were perfectly safe from attack by the Varela's boats. They cursed, fumed and threatened, but nothing would bring the necessary implements from the depths of the sea and finally, clapping all of the crew in irons, they headed for Fayal.

Here an American warship was met and after a preliminary examination eight of the Varela's men were placed aboard the man-o'-war in irons and were brought to the United States for trial. No similar "mutiny" had ever before occurred, and as the men had not openly refused to obey orders, had not threatened or attacked the officers, and as only circumstantial evidence was forthcoming, the Court was in a quandary. The sentence finally passed upon the "mutineers" was perhaps the most amusing part of the whole affair, for each of the eight men who had been transported in a United States warship in irons received the remarkable sentence of ten days in jail.

But of all perils which beset the whaleman the danger of being crushed in the ice was probably the greatest and more ships were lost by ice than by all other causes combined. On two occasions, in 1871 and in 1876, entire fleets were lost in the ice of the Arctic – twenty vessels being destroyed in 1876 while the disaster of 1871 was the greatest catastrophe which ever befell the whaling industry, thirty-two vessels being destroyed, leaving over twelve hundred persons shipwrecked and causing a monetary loss of over one million dollars to New Bedford alone.

In one respect also it stands forth as the most remarkable of maritime disasters, for despite the number of vessels destroyed, the number of shipwrecked people, and the rigors and dangers they faced, not a single life was lost.

It was early in May 1871, that the Arctic whaling fleet gathered on the grounds south of Cape Thaddeus where the ice was closely packed by a strong wind blowing from the northeast. By June, foggy weather set in with light variable winds and, the ice opening, the ships passed through and came in sight of Cape Navarre where five or six whales were taken and many others were seen spouting amid the ice. By the middle of June the ice had opened still more and the fleet pressed on through the Anadir Sea, capturing more whales, and by the thirtieth of the month had passed Behring Strait, following the whales.

Through July the vessels continued whaling and when in the latter part of that month the ice drifted from the eastern shores of Cape Lisborne the fleet turned to the east and followed the ice and worked through open leads until within a few miles of Icy Cape. Here some of the ships dropped anchor, owing to the ice which prevented them from reaching Blossom Shoals, but by August 6, the ice receded and several vessels got under way and a few days later most of the fleet was north of the shoals and had worked to the northeast as far as Wainwright Inlet where eight ships came to anchor or fastened to the ice and whaling proceeded briskly.

On August 11, however, the wind suddenly shifted and set the ice inshore, catching several boats which were cruising for whales in the open ice and forcing the ships to get under way. Although several of the boats were stove they were all saved by hauling them over the ice and the ships sought shelter close inshore under the lee of the ground ice. On August 13 they managed to work through open strips of water to Point Belcher where they waited for a northeast wind to blow the ice off.

But instead of coming from the northeast, as expected, the wind came from the west, driving the ice-pack inshore and forcing the ships into a narrow strip of water about half a mile wide and close to the land. Here they remained, with ice stretching for twenty miles along the coast, but whales were abundant, and their capture was still continued, the whales being cut in from the ice and the blubber carried over the ice to the ships.

On August 25, the expected northeast wind arrived blowing a gale and driving the ice four to eight miles offshore, and the Eskimos vainly endeavored to induce the whalemen to take advantage of the open water. Four days later the wind shifted, the ice again drove inshore, and several vessels were caught in the floes, while the others retreated until the immense masses of ice grounded in shallow water. The first disaster occurred on September 2, when the *Comet* was caught and crushed, the crew, however, escaping to the other vessels. Each day the ice drew closer, pushed inshore by the ceaseless southerly and westerly winds, and on the seventh of September the bark *Roman* was caught and crushed between two floes. The next day the *Awashonks* met the same fate, and realizing ,their predicament the crews were set to work building up the gunwales of the boats and sheathing them with copper to protect them from the ice, which now extended unbroken for eighty miles.

A boat was then sent south to search for other vessels, and upon its return reported that the *Arctic* and six other ships were still clear and would stand by to receive the fugitives if they abandoned their ships. As it appeared hopeless for the vessels to escape, the boats were provisioned, the flags set union-down upon the ships and on September 14, the flotilla of boats, loaded with men and with several women and children among them, set forth on their hazardous attempt to reach the vessels eighty miles distant beyond the icepack.

At the close of the first day the boats landed on the beach at the foot of some sandhills and here camp was made, the boats being turned up and sails stretched over them as shelter for the women and children. By the second day Blossom Shoals were reached and beyond a tongue of ice the waiting ships could be seen about five miles distant, but a gale was blowing, a heavy sea was running, and the icy wind froze the spray wherever it touched.

Protected by the jutting ice it was bad enough, but as soon as the end of this was passed the waves became mountainous, the boats constantly shipped water, the provisions were soaked and ruined and the occupants, drenched to the skin, were compelled to bail for their lives. So tremendous were the waves and so heavy the gale that the great anchor-chain of the Arctic snapped as if made of thread and yet the tiny boats bore on, the men never faltering, the women never complaining, and despite the furious Arctic tempest reached the tossing ships in safety.

Think of it – twelve hundred and nineteen souls rowing through storm-lashed, ice-filled seas for nearly one hundred miles in open boats and not a man, woman or child missing when at last the refuge of the ships was gained! Surely a record to be proud of and a feat that proved to all the world the heroism, gallantry and courage of the whalemen!

7 - THE LOG OF THE WHALEMAN

LIKE ALL OTHER SEAMEN the whalemen had their log-books, and in these many a thrilling story of adventure, many a marvelous escape from death, and many a strange tale of the sea lie hidden. On a merchant ship the logs were kept more as a matter of course than anything else, and as a rule are dry reading, for entries of wind and weather, the courses and distances sailed and such items are about all they contain. Not so with the logs of the whalemen, however. Aside from the weather, the winds, the latitude and longitude and other matters of a similar sort the whalers' logs contained accounts of all the whales attacked or taken, the amount of oil or bone obtained and the strange people and stranger places visited. Everything which was done aboard ship or ashore was set down in quaint, terse sentences and curiously mis-spelled words and no event of importance was overlooked.

To the whaling captains the logs were of vast importance and upon the margins of the pages and on the blank leaves they jotted memoranda, did sums in arithmetic, wrote letters and made comments which are often as interesting as the true contents of the log itself. There was no rush and hurry about writing the log on a whaleship – time was the most abundant of all things – and the mates and captains often wrote their logs as they would a letter or a story. Often, too, they illustrated the entries in the logbooks with pen-and-ink sketches, and if an officer had talent and an artistic temperament, as often happened, the books were decorated with full-page colored drawings and paintings.

Some of these showed the ship under full sail, others depicted the chase and capture of whales and still others represented scenes in foreign lands and gave a far better idea of the places visited, the adventures met and the events of the cruise than the written words.

Even when not really illustrated and decorated in such a manner the logbooks were filled with pictures showing the whales attacked, caught, killed and lost, for the whalers found "picture-writing" far easier and more satisfactory than setting down numerous items in script. Sometimes the crude pictures of the whales were drawn with a pen, but as a rule they were made by means of stamps, carved from wood by the men themselves, while in recent years rubber stamps have been used.

Whenever an entry regarding a whale was to be made, the impression of the proper stamp was made on the margin of the page and thus, at a glance, the reader could determine how many whales were taken, how many escaped, and how many barrels of oil each furnished, for the number of barrels of oil was written on a small, blank spot left upon the likeness of each whale for that purpose.

Some of the whalers used plain, black ink on the stamps, but others made the miniature whales in brilliant blue and added a realistic touch. by painting on a plume of scarlet spray to show the creatures were killed and "spouted blood." As many of the whalers cruised both for sperm and right whales there were stamps for each kind and even porpoises and grampuses were not forgotten and some of the old logs look like veritable marine menageries with their black, blue and red whales, grampuses, porpoises, walruses and seals scattered over the pages. In addition to the logbooks there were the journals and diaries kept by the officers and even by members of the crew, and these often contained matters of far more interest to the world at large than the real logs.

Of course, many of the old logs and journals were destroyed, many were tucked away in chests and garrets never again to be brought forth, while still others were preserved either by the whalemen or their families or by individuals interested in the whaling industry. By a perusal of these old ships' books one may get a better insight of the whalemen's lives than by any other means, for the entries often reflected the hopes, sorrows, joys and sentiments of the whalemen to a wonderful degree. Sometimes the story of a burial at sea will be recorded; again the birthday of the captain, the anniversary of his wedding or other family events will be set down in heavy underscored lines, while not infrequently some trivial event – such as the killing of a chicken for dinner or the fact that the "old sow had six pigs" will be duly entered and illustrated with as much care and seriousness as the staving of a boat or the taking of a hundred-barrel whale.

Some of the logs were filled with laments and sadness from beginning to end, others were redolent of happiness and jollity; some told of long voyages with nothing but empty casks and disappointments as a result, while still others were obviously written by men on the verge of madness or by religious fanatics.

Among the older logs some are very quaint and one, dated in 1745, states that it is the record of "A Journey by God's Permission in the *Nazarene* from Virginia to Whithaven."

Another remarkable log was kept by Captain Clothier Pierce of the *Minnesota*, a man who wept over his log whenever he opened it and headed every page with the caption: "Remarks on Board the Most Unfortunate Vessel in the Whaling Business." His shipmates must have had a mighty melancholy time on their cruises, for he did nothing but lament continually and his daily entries in the logbook were as lugubrious as the headings to the pages – as illustrated by the following extracts:

"July 1, 1868. No signs of life here, nothing for us. June has passed and we get nowhere. No chance for us this season I fear. Three seasons in the North Atlantic to get one whale in this unfortunate vessel.

"July 4th, Wind E. S. E. Will the wind never change? This is the Fourth of July a day of rejoicing with People at

Home. But a sad day for us. No whales in the ocean that we can find. A head wind. No chance to do anything or to ever get one whale. "The Lord's Hand appears to be against the poor old *Minnesota* and all concerned in her. Will the Lord in his infinite Mercy ever suffer us to get one Whale? Employed sheathing the deck. Many are rejoicing today but our hearts are filled with sadness that this poor vessel cannot get a whale."

"July 12th. Nothing to be seen but sails I fear the ocean contains no treasures for this unfortunate vessel. Nothing like sperm whales here. Picked up a barrel of petroleum oil. So the time passes and we get nothing.

"July 13th. No whale this season for the poor old *Minnesota*. The Lord will not suffer us to get one I am so wicked..."

Under other dates this sad captain entered such sentiments as the following:

"Fate I fear has ordained that we get nothing this season. May the Lord in His mercy pour out a blessing for this unfortunate vessel is my earnest prayer although I feel I am unworthy."

"May that being that presides over the destinies of men guide and direct me in all things I desire. Some fog, bad weather for seeing. A perfect desert. The Pierce family are unfortunate. Looks desolate. Our ruin is inevitable."

One really pities this man after reading over the log he wrote so many years ago and it brings a sigh of relief to learn that despite his forebodings he succeeded in taking some whales before his voyage was over. Some of the old skippers and their mates imagined they possessed literary talent and quite often varied the monotony of their logbook entries by scraps of impromptu verse. Most of this was mere doggerel, but now and then some man left evidence of real talent and at times wrote parodies on well-known poems or songs which were quite amusing. Such a man was the steward of the *Emmeline*, one Washington Foster, who kept the log of the schooner on a voyage from Mystic,

Connecticut to the Croisettes, on a cruise for sea-elephant oil. His parody on "The Old Oaken Bucket" was not bad for a whaleman and his entry for Christmas day was quite a literary masterpiece for a whaleship's logbook. I quote both verbatim as follows:

"How dear to this heart are the scenes of past days.

"When fond recollection recalls them to mind.

"The schooner so taut and so trim like a miss in her stays.

"And all her light rigging which swayed to the wind.

"The old-fashioned galley, the try-works close by it.

"The old blubber boat with six oars to pull it.

"The bunk of my messmate, the wooden chest nigh it.

"The old Monkey jacket, the often-patched jacket.

"The greasy old jacket which hung up beside it."

"Monday Dec. 25th. 1843. Begins with strong winds with hail and rain from NW to NNW. Had an early breakfast and watched a favorable opportunity for starting to the shore at half past 4 A.M. The wind lulling a little the boat put off taking with them a bag of bread for the shore party and in a few minutes arrived at the beach. We had almost forgotten that today is Christmas day, the season of festivity and rejoicing at home and we can almost fancy that we hear the halls resounding with the enlivening notes of the violin and the merry step of the fascinating dance, the tables groaning under the weight of poultry, pies and all the delicacies of the season, and – but stop, the bark of that infernal sea elephant has destroyed the illusion and recalled our wandering senses back to our anchorage in the cold, stormy, cheerless and desolate Croisettes. But no matter, 'tis true we cannot at present revel amid the strong, exhilarating mixtures and quaff the luxurious wines of the seasons, being at present all hands of us, 'teetotalers' – but we can look forward to St. Helena and a full ship and in sweet anticipation lay back in a bottle of Cunningham's best and that is almost as good as though we had it. Moreover we can, – listen to me now, ye epicures who ransack ocean, earth and air to satisfy your pampered and vitiated appetites, – we live, nay we feast, here in this remote and dismal corner of the globe on luxuries the savory flavor of which you can form no conception. The richest and most delicious morsels of food that ever found its way into human stomach, such as sea elephant's tongues, flippers, hearts, livers tripe, etc., so that we are not so bad off during the holidays, but that we might be much worse." Surely a man capable of writing matter such as the above was worthy of a better fate than serving as a greasy steward aboard a whaler. The old logbook which contains his verses and his descriptive entries smells abominably of guano, although more than seventy years have passed since the Emmeline sold her sea-elephant oil in Cape Town and sailed to Ichaboe Island to load guano[19] for home.

Tales of trouble with the crew, of leaks, of good and bad luck, of storm and other events are common, but only now and then is a logbook found which contains accounts of a mutiny, for the excellent reason that when a crew mutinied and took the ship the logbooks were usually destroyed. The log of the Junior is still preserved, as already mentioned, and the log of the Barclay, from which the following extracts were taken, also relates the story of a mutiny.

The Barclay's log belongs to Andrew Snow, Jr. of Padanaram, Massachusetts, who has a remarkable collection of old whaling logs, journals and other relics of the industry. The logs of the Emmeline and the Minnesota, quoted above, and that of the Morea, to be mentioned later, are also in Mr. Snow's collection.

The memorable voyage of the ship Barclay began on September 13, 1834, and ended on September 27, 1837, and the thrilling incidents with which it was replete might

---

[19] Peat-like bird excrement used for fuel.

well form the basis for a fascinating tale of the sea. Trouble commenced on the Barclay very soon after leaving port, although nothing very tragic materialized for some time, but as an example of the manner in which logs were kept, the first entries on the *Barclay*'s log are interesting.

"Saturday on board. Lying at anchor, Bedford Harbor below Palmer's Is. 5 fathoms of water. First part of these 24 hours strong breezes from the NW, the weather fine. Most of the crew on board employed in Ship's Duty. Mid part (of the day) light airs from the N.W. Latt. part a fine breeze from the N. At 5 o'clock broke ground and bid adieu to the land we all so much admire. But with the hopes of a short voyage, we set sail. At 9 o'clock the pilot left us. Steered out SW. At 11 o'clock the wind shifted to the east from that time to the SE, we steering to the SW. At 12 o'clock to Gay Head lighthouse. Bore E 1-2 N. Dist. 8 miles. The No Mans Land Bore ESE. Saw number of vessels steering different courses. So ends this day with sweet feelings of Home."

Although each day's entry in a log closed with "So ends this day" yet the above termination of a day's entries is very unusual. The next entry of note in this log of the *Barclay* is dated "Monday Oct. the 6th."

"Commenced with fine Weather and light Winds from the South. We with all sails set. One brig in sight at 2 o'clock. Lowered our boats to exercise the crew, which was very necessary. At supper while in the act of sharing the vittals forward, one of the crew began to fight with some of the Green hands, it being the third time. We put him in rigging not intending to flay him but his saucy tongue caused him a few stripes with fore parts of a small headline after which he acknowledged he was to blame. We then let him go forward where he made number of threats. This promising youth's name is Bradford Trafford. Mid part light airs from the South. The Blacksmiths very saucy he being the worse for Rum. Latt. part calmer, lowered the boats and chased grampus for whales."

"Oct. the 8th. Nothing to be seen but the wide Ocean. Our old Rigging parts very often, it is not otherwise to be expected. So ends this long and Dismal day in hopes of a fare one."

But the "fare" weather was not to be and the voyage was rough and the weather stormy and "Heavy Gails" lasted for days as the ship labored and wallowed round Cape Horn and into the Pacific. No entries were made on many days on account of the heavy weather necessitating the captain's presence constantly on deck and even Christmas Day and New Years were passed over without an observation. Once in the Pacific, however, matters improved and entries were again made and under date of "Friday, April the 29th." the following occurs.

"At 8 o'clock the Captain sent the steward forward to call the men aft or one of them, to see their meat weighed; but their reply was that they would not come. This was told the Captain. He immediately called to them to come aft and repeated it three times and then went after them and took a broom at one of the blacks. They all refused to go aft but one said one of their complaint was that one pound and ¼ of meat was not enough and were very insolent and made their threats. They now went forward not wishing to see their weight of meat. The said black was insolent to the Captain when coming forward but was called to go aft again, his reply was that he would not and fled for the forecastle. While getting him up one of the men Henry Ketchum came at the gangway and interfered and challenged the Captain and struck him. At this time the Captain took hold of him and dropped his weapon. The fellow took it up and made an attempt to strike the Captain with it. From this he was told to go aft but refused and went down the forecastle. Took a sheath knife and said he would kill the first man that went down but afterward delivered himself to be put in irons where now remains in the Run, thus ends in peace."

Fortunately for the *Barclay* the mutiny was nipped in the bud, and whales soon being sighted, the crew forgot their troubles in the hard and exciting work of the chase, but no doubt things looked serious indeed on that memorable Friday in April and the strangely punctuated and spelled words, with their oddly placed capital letters, give but a vague impression of the exciting hours when the handful of officers faced their sullen, mutinous crew and stared death in the face.

In a former chapter, I mentioned the fact that captains at times became maniacs through loneliness, and allowing their thoughts to dwell constantly on matters of religion, and the log of the New Bedford ship *Morea* records such a case.

The *Morea* left New Bedford on October 13, 1853, and returned on May 1, 1856, and here it is interesting to note that while whalers apparently had little superstitious dread of setting forth on the thirteenth, yet both the *Barclay* and the *Morea*, as well as several other vessels, on which tragedies occurred, set sail on the thirteenth day of the month. The earliest entries on the *Morea's* logs are of little interest and were made by the captain, Thomas B. Peabody, but the later entries, after June 1854, and which were made by the chief mate, Beriah C. Manchester, relate a sad and tragic story of the sea.

"'Remarks on board the ship *Morea*, Sat. June 3d. 1854.

"Strong winds from WNW and some fog. The first part ship head SE. Saw five ships. This afternoon Captain Peabody retired for a while and on being called at the tea table he made some very unusual remarks from him to make, asking the officers if they thought a man would be punished in the other world for making away with himself if he had nothing to hope for or could see no prospect of happiness before him. At night he went to bed as usual and was up during the night giving directions how to steer. At breakfast he seemed rather melancholy, ate but little and after breakfast came on deck but soon went below again. At 10 A. M. he sent the Steward after me to come below. I went into the cabin. He was in his berth. He told me he had sent for me to tell me that he was going to meet his god and gave me his reasons for so doing, and some little directions about his things. After conversing with him for some twenty minutes or more I went on deck and communicated that he had told me to the other officers.

"Soon after we three – the second and third mates and myself – went down and inquired if he had taken anything to cause him to be as he was. At first he said no, only a spoonful of brandy but soon after on being asked again he said he would not go with a lie for he had taken laudanum; but as we thought he had not taken enough to cause death we let him be. He now inquired how the weather was. At meridian he got up, called for a light, lit a cigar and went to bed again. So, this affair stood at noon. Middle and last of this day fresh SW winds and cloudy weather, etc. One man sick.

"Remarks Sunday June 4th. 1854.

"Strong South winds and some rain etc. At 2 p.m. Capt. Peabody got up and wanted an observation taken but he was in such a state he was not able to note the time. He remained up till 6.30 p.m. while up gave his opinion on the prospect of whales at certain places then went to bed again.

"At 9 p.m., he gave orders to lay the head yards back. At 2.30. a.m., he gave orders to steer north as soon as it was light enough to man the masthead. At breakfast he said he could not eat anything. He seemed in his right mind through the forenoon. At dinner time I asked him if he could eat some dinner. He said the thoughts of food made him sick to his stomach but said the steward was going to make some soup, etc.

"Monday June 5th, 1854. About 2 P.M. saw two whales. Lowered three boats. At 3 returned on board without getting fast. While the boats was off Capt. Peabody gave orders to make more sail and keep the ship near the boats and after we got on board he asked me how many whales I saw. At teatime he was in bed and did not get up. At 6.30 p.m. saw two whales the weather too thick to lower. While looking at the whales there being no one in the cabin but the captain, we heard the report of a gun and a musket ball come through the deck. We immediately went below and found Capt. Peabody lying on deck in his room with his face blown off from his chin to his eyes both upper and lower jaws entirely off. He breathed a few moments and was gone. Middle part more moderate. At 1.30 a.m. saw ice, then to rest. At 8.30 a.m. committed the remains of Captain Peabody to the deep, and a solemn night it was indeed. Thus ends these 24 hours."

It is something of a relief to turn from these plain, unvarnished, laboriously written tales of sad or tragic events to the ordinary logs relating pleasant voyages, good catches and full cargoes, of which the following are typical examples.

"Remarks on Board the ship *Ohio* of Nantucket. Chas. W. Coffin, Master. Cruising off Japan.

"Friday July 17, 1834.
"First part light breezes at S.W. Lie up N.E. under full sail employed repairing the foretopmast and staysail finished bent it wet the hold. At sunset shortened sail. Middle part much the same at daylight commenced stowing down at 9 a.m. Saw a shoal of sperm whales. Put off at 11 A.M. struck, the boats among whales. N. Lat. 31."
The crude imprints on the margins of the page indicate that three whales were taken, one was "mist" and one "drew iron."

"Remarks on Board of the Ship *Montreal* in the Kamchatka Sea. F. L. Fish, Master.

"Thursday July the 15th. 1851.

"These 24 hours commenced with a light air and cloudy from the southwards and westward the boats off chasing whales, at 3 P.M. struck 2 whales and turned them up 7 miles from the ship and commenced towing them to the ship in a calm at 11 took them alongside with fresh breeze and rain from the S at 1 A.M. all hands sent below at 7 called all hands and commenced cutting in, latter part puffy with a light air and a berg, heavy swell from the S all hands employed in cutting. At 12 M. had one whale in and hooked on to the other. So ends. Lat, 60 53' North."

Throughout every page of these two logs, and many others as well, the entries are much the same: good weather, plenty of whales, constant employment, and casks steadily filled with oil. Such were the ordinary events of a whaling cruise, and while most of the ships filled up and made good catches, now and then a vessel had poor luck and returned from a long cruise without getting enough oil "to grease their boots" as one whaleman expressed it. Usually this was due to the fault of the whalers themselves and such was the case on the bark *Alexander*, which sailed in 1835 and whose journal – in the possession of Mr. P. H. Nye – is one of the most curious and amusing records of a whaling cruise ever written.

From first to last this remarkable voyage was scarcely more than one continuous orgy on the part of the officers. The captain and mates spent all of their waking hours in drinking, discipline was thrown entirely aside and, as the entries in the journal show, there was scarcely a day when the skipper and his mates were not drunk. Indeed the journal – kept by the cooper Ephraim Billings – served as a log-book of the cruise, for the captain and mates were usually too intoxicated to think of the log – much less to write any account of the daily happenings, which was perhaps a bit of wisdom on their part, for if they had jotted down the truth it would have been far-from creditable to themselves.

The poor cooper must have had a hard and dismal time of it, as proved by his quaint entries and remarks, while nearly every page ended with "May God have mercy on this ship," "God knows what will become of us all," "May God grant this voyage soon ends," or "Thank God another day has passed."

For a time the cooper made daily notes on the condition of the captain and the officers and stated that, "The captain was middling drunk," "All hands came aboard drunk," "The mates were very drunk," etc., but he soon gave this up in despair and as of too frequent occurrence and confined himself to recording the times when more unusual conditions occurred, as, "Captain only a little drunk," "Some hands sober," "Mates not very drunk," or "Captain not drunk today." Only once did he enter anything to the captain's credit. This was on an occasion when an insolent and rebellious "boy" of the ship's company was thrashed by the captain and Ephraim remarks "This is the best deed the captain has done on this terrible voyage. Pray God he may repeat the work often."

No doubt Billings was terribly homesick, for he was the only man who remained sober and gave a thought to the welfare of the bark and he never failed to note the anniversary of his birth, of his marriage, or of the death of his wife throughout the voyage and underscored such entries with heavy, black lines.

Funnily enough the cooper never wrote his journal in the first person, but always as if speaking of another, as, "This day is the birthday of Ephraim Billings, cooper[20] of the bark *Alexander*, or "The cooper, Ephraim Billings, remained on board, all others being ashore drunk."

---

[20] Barrel maker.

The poor man's troubles finally came to an end when the captain had him arrested for mutiny in a South American port, the "mutiny" consisting of appearing on deck in his stocking feet. The South American prison was far from a punishment, however, for the cooper found it a most welcome change from the ship. When he became sober the captain endeavored to induce Ephraim to return to the vessel, but the cooper had had enough of it, and in his journal states that he refused, "As God knows I know too much of what goes on and what I may expect." According to his journal Billings had a very easy and pleasant time, on shore, for he was released from prison, was entertained by the officials and finally reached home in safety, "Never to go a whaling again, please God."

THE WHALERS' CHANTEY MIGHT truthfully be said to typify their life, fully half of which consisted mainly of kicks. But if their work was hard, their food coarse and none too plentiful, their calling dangerous and their treatment often brutal, yet they had their hours of leisure when all their hardships and perils were forgotten.

Aboard their ships idle moments were occupied by mending their worn clothes, carving curios or other articles from bone or whales' teeth or doing "scrimshaw"[21] work. There is an old saying among sailors that a "whaleman can be told by his patches" and at the close of a long cruise the whalers' garments were more patches than anything else, often consisting of "holes with a few rags around them" or a "patch upon patch and a patch over all " – this term being applied to a peculiar method used by the whalers for getting the utmost possible service out of their clothing. By placing one garment within another, sewing them together and patching any rents or openings which happened to coincide, two absolutely worthless articles of wearing apparel could be combined to form one wearable garment.

When both of the articles were dark colored the effect was not so bad – if the work was well done – but when one was light and the other dark, or when a pair of red drawers was used as the foundation for dark trousers, the effect was striking to say the least and it is not to be wondered at that whalemen were famed for their patches throughout the maritime world. Scrimshaw work was a term applied to all forms of carving or decorating whales' teeth, walrus' tusks or bones, but nowadays usually refers specifically to the teeth engraved by the whalemen. Some of the men

---

[21] Scrollwork, engravings, and carvings done in bone or ivory.

became very expert in carving and decorating the teeth and tusks and produced marvelously delicate and beautiful handiwork with the crudest of tools, or even with a jack-knife alone. In decorating the teeth the design was scratched upon the smooth, hard surface and colors, such as India ink, paint, or even soot from the try-works, was rubbed into the incised lines.

By this laborious and crude method results equaling the finest steel engravings were often produced, although the majority of scrimshawed teeth showed little artistic talent on the part of the men. Many of the designs were original, such as ships under full sail, incidents of the chase and capture of whales and other maritime scenes, but the best and most elaborate were traced or transferred from the books, magazines or illustrated papers which found their way to the forecastles of the whaling ships.

More ambitious and skillful members of the crews carved articles from the teeth and their cribbage boards, made from walrus tusks, the beautifully inlaid boxes of whalebone, ivory, shell and wood and many articles manufactured by the whalemen from the materials at hand were as delicately carved, as well finished and as intricate in design as any work of the Orient.[22]

More numerous than all other articles made by the whalers were the odd "jagging wheels" for crimping the edges of pastry, pies, etc. No one seems to know just why the whalemen were so fond of making these, but it may have been due to ever-present thoughts of the delicious pies of their New England homes and which for years at a time were but memories of the past or expectations of the future.

Whatever the reason, the carved pastry wheels were produced in vast numbers by the whalemen and many were most ingenious in construction and were most

---

[22] Most were disposable, only a tiny percentage of scrimshaw examples show artistic talent.

beautifully wrought. The best collection of these in existence is that of the Old Dartmouth Historical Society of New Bedford and whole cases filled with this handiwork of the whalemen may be seen in the Society's museum.

Many of the wheels were highly ornamented with mother-of-pearl, whalebone or brass wire inlaid in the ivory; others were intricately carved, while one specimen is made entirely of tortoise shell. Nearly everyone bears a fork at one end for piercing the pie-crust or the cake, and in some cases the fork is so arranged as to fold down, while in other instances two, three, five or even seven wheels of various sizes are combined on one instrument. Looking at these examples of the whalemen's skill one marvels at the time and patience which must have been required to cut them with a jack-knife from the dense, hard teeth, but time was no object and often hung heavy on the whalers' hands, and men who hunted whales on three- or five-year cruises possessed patience to the utmost degree.

But of all amusements or recreations, other than shore-leave, the whalers looked forward with the greatest anticipation to "gamming." To "gam" meant to visit another ship and whenever two vessels met at sea, and the weather would permit, they were hove-to and hours were spent in gamming.

The whalemen had their own ideas of etiquette, and these were observed with as much formality as on a man-o'-war. When going gamming the captain of one ship had the starboard boat lowered and was pulled to the other vessel while her mate returned the visit in the larboard boat. If both the vessels hailed from the same port there were letters to be sent home or received, inquiries about friends and relatives to be made, comparisons of catches and cargoes, stories of adventures to be told and innumerable healths to be drunk, for a "gam" called for spirits, food, tobacco and other forms of celebration in the forecastle, as well as in the cabin.

If, however, one ship was a "sound boat" and the other an "island" or Nantucket vessel, each of the crews would strive to outdo the other in their yarns and stories – as well as in profanity – for there was keen rivalry between the vessels hailing from New Bedford, New London and other coast ports and those from Nantucket, and the men were never so happy as when they could boast of a bigger catch or of more oil than their rivals. But whether rivals or friends good-fellowship prevailed while the gamming continued; the forecastles and cabins rang with laughter, the decks resounded to the shuffle and patter of dancing feet and lusty lungs roared forth the whalemen's songs.

Many of these songs of the whalemen were very descriptive of their lives, their experiences and their hardships; others were sentimental; still others were comic, or contained "flings" at captains and officers, while the great majority of them – if the truth must be confessed – were indescribably obscene or terribly profane.

Chanteys too were sung by the whalemen, but unlike the songs their chanteys were identical with those known to seamen the world over and which have been handed down by word of mouth since the days of Drake[23] and Rodney.[24] Often, to be sure, the whalers varied the words of the chanteys to suit their own particular needs, but the airs remained the same as those chorused by the crews of merchant ships.

Like the merchantmen, the whaleships had their "chantey-men," old hands who knew every working song of the five oceans, and the chantey-man on a whaler was almost as much of a privileged character and as great a favorite with the men as his prototype on a merchant vessel. It was his duty to start the songs going, as the crew hove at windlass or tailed to brace or halyard, and often he did little more than sing his way through a cruise, for

---

[23] English explorer and circumnavigator of the globe, Sir Francis Drake (c.1540-1596).
[24] Admiral George Brydges Rodney, 1st Baron Rodney, (1718-1792).

his chanteys put such life and vigor in the men that officers could afford to overlook his shirking at times.

There is nothing which excels a rousing song in making hard work light, and the value of a good chantey was appreciated by men and officers alike. Oftentimes the men found an opportunity to vent their pent-up feelings and to express their opinions of ship, officers, and life in general in their songs and chanteys and with practical immunity from punishment. Many a hard-fisted mate and brutal skipper has smiled at the descriptions of his own shortcomings in chantey or song when the same words, if spoken, would result in a blow from a belaying-pin or a dose of the "cat" for the man who had the temerity to express such sentiments. Although the chanteys were often improvised by the chantey-man and the words varied, yet the airs were always the same and certain chanteys were always used for definite purposes. There were anchor, or capstan chanteys; halyard chanteys and sheet; tack or bowline chanteys; and the clank and clatter of capstan-pawls, the creak of windlass, or the squeak and groan of yards and tackle-blocks were invariably accompanied by some chantey or song roared boisterously from the whalemen's throats.

Many a time the familiar air of "Whiskey Johnny" helped the men as they hauled at the halyards, and as the great sails were hoisted and the ship spread her white wings these words rang out across the waves:

Oh, whiskey is the life of man,
Whiskey! Johnny!
It always was since time began,
Oh, whiskey for my Johnny!
Oh, whiskey makes me wear old clo's,
Whiskey! Johnny!
'Twas whiskey gave me a broken nose,
Oh, whiskey for my Johnny!
I think I heard our Old Man say,

Whiskey! Johnny!
"I'll treat my men in a decent way,"
Oh, whiskey for my Johnny!
"I'll treat my men in a decent way,"
Whiskey! Johnny!
"I'll grog them all three times a day,"
Oh, whiskey for my Johnny!
"A glass of grog for every man,"
Whiskey! Johnny!
"And a bottle full for the Chantey Man,"
Oh, whiskey for my Johnny! Or again it may have been
"Hanging Johnny," which aided in spreading topsails to
the wind and above the thrash of unfurled canvas and the
rattle of blocks one would hear:
They call me Hanging Johnny,
Away – e – Oh!
They call me Hanging Johnny,
So hang, boys, hang.
I'll hang you all together,
Away – e – Oh!
I'll hang you all together,
So hang, boys, hang.

Then, as the crew bent to the handspikes and the great
anchor came slowly from the ground the chantey-man
would roar out the words and the men would join lustily
in the chorus of some well-known chantey, such as "The
Rio Grande," "A Maid of Amsterdam," or "The Fishes " –
the last being particularly appropriate for the whalemen:

Oh, a ship she was rigged and ready for sea,
Windy weather! Stormy-weather!
And all of her sailors were fishes to be,
Blow ye winds, westerly, gentle sou'westerly,
Blow ye winds westerly, – steady she goes.

Oh, first came the herring, the king o' the sea,
Windy weather! Stormy weather!
He jumped on the poop. "I'll be capt'n!" cried he.
Blow ye winds westerly, gentle sou'westerly
Blow ye winds westerly, – steady she goes!

Oh, next came a flatfish, they call him a skate,
Windy weather! Stormy weather!
"If you be the capt'n why sure I'm the mate."
Blow ye winds westerly, gentle sou'westerly,
Blow ye winds westerly, – steady she goes.

As the to'gallant sails were hoisted the song changed
to a different air and the welkin rang to:

And who d'ye think's the skipper o' her?
Blow, boys, blow!
Why, Holy Joe, the nigger lover!
Blow, my bully boys, blow!

Now who d' ye think's the chief mate o' her?
Blow, boys, blow!
A big mu-latter come from Antigua!
Blow, my bully boys, blow!

And what d'ye think we had for dinner?
Blow, boys, blow!
Mosquito's heart and sandfly's liver,
Blow, my bully boys, blow!

Chanteys with a chorus of "Blow, my bully boys, blow"
were very common and were always favorites with whalemen and merchant sailors alike and innumerable
chanteys have a chorus of these or similar words; as for
example the two following:

Oh, blow ye winds I long to have you,

Blow, bullies, blow!
Oh, blow today and blow tomorrow,
Blow, my bully boys, blow!

Oh, blow today and blow tomorrow,
Blow, bullies, blow!
Oh, blow away all care and sorrow,
Blow, my bully boys, blow!

...

As I was a-walking down Paradise Street,
Away – hay – blow the man down;
A trim little packet I happened to meet.
Oh, give us some time to blow a man down.

I hailed her in English, she answered me clear
Away – hay – blow the man down;
"I'm from the Black Anchor bound to the Shake-speare,"
Oh, give us some time to blow a man down!

So I tailed her my flipper and took her in tow,
Away – hay – blow the man down;
And yardarm to yardarm away we did go.
Oh, give us some time to blow a man down!

But unfortunately for Jack the "trim little packet" al-ways proved to be a pirate sailing under false colors, according to the chantey-man's verses, and, after reciting the adventures which befell him upon taking the deceptive young woman "in tow," the singer would proceed to preach a sermon in chantey-form and warned all his fellows in the following words:

Now I'll give you a warning afore we belay,
Away – hay – blow the man down!

Don't never pay heed to what pretty gals say,
Oh, give us some time to blow the man down!

Or again the tune might be that of "Cape Horn" and
the leather-lunged chantey-man would lead the crews at
their labor with:

I wish to God I'd never been born,
To me way, – hay, hay – yah
To go sailing round and round Cape Horn,
A long time ago – !

Around Cape Horn, where wild gales blow,
To me way, – hay, hay – yah!
Around Cape Horn through sleet and snow,
A long time ago – !

Around Cape Horn with frozen sails,
To me way, – hay, hay – yah!
Around Cape Horn to hunt for whales,
A long time ago – !

"Sally Brown" was also a favorite chantey and the Yankee whalemen carried the words and air of this splendid
sea song into the uttermost parts of the world. In the
South Seas the Kanakas chant it as they labor; in the
palm-fringed isles of the Caribbean the chorus rings me-
lodiously from the throats of the toiling negroes hauling
logs or pulling drougher-boats,[25] for wherever the whalemen touched the natives caught the air, – often with no
knowledge of the meaning of the words – and through generations it has come down, usually garbled and
unintelligible, but always recognizable.

Oh, Sally Brown of New York City,

---

[25] A fast support boat designed to be carried aboard a larger vessel.

Aye Sally, – Sally Brown,
Of pretty Sal this is a ditty,
I'll spend my money on Sally Brown!

Oh, Sally Brown is a white man's daughter,
Aye, Sally, – Sally Brown.
Oh, Sally Brown is very pretty.
I'll spend my money on Sally Brown!

But stirring as the chanteys were, when roared in me-
lodious unison from a score of hairy throats, yet they were
not typical of the whalemen and came second-hand from
the deep-sea sailors of the merchant marine – and often
sadly worn and in bad shape at that. Indeed few of an outward bound whaleship's crew had ever heard a chantey or
even knew the meaning of the word, and while the "greenies" soon picked up the songs and chanteys of their more
experienced comrades the chorus on an outward-bound
whaler was often pitifully weak.

What they lacked in their chanteys was made up for in
their songs, however, and one might obtain a very fair idea
of the whalemen's lives and duties, how the whales were
caught, and the hardships of the whalers' calling from
their songs alone.

For example, nothing could be truer to life than the
following, which was an old stand-by and no doubt gave
the singer much relief, when he realized what a fool he'd
made of himself by shipping on a whaling vessel.

'Twas advertised in Boston,
New York and Buffalo,
Five hundred brave Americans,
A-whaling for to go.

They send you to New Bedford,
The famous whaling port;
They send you to a shark's store,

And board and fit you out.

They send you to a boarding-house,
For a time to dwell.
The thieves there, they are thicker
Than the other side of hell.

They tell you of the whaling ships,
A-going in and out.
They swear you'll make your fortune
Before you're five months out.

But now we're out at sea, my boys,
We find life hard enough.
A little piece of stinking meat
And a blamed small bag of duff.

Next comes the running rigging,
Which we're all supposed to know.
'Tis "Lay aloft, you son-of-a-gun,
Or overboard you go."

The capt'ns on the quarter-deck,
A-squintin' at the sails,
Aloft four men are standin',
A-searchin' for sperm whales.

The cooper at his vise bench
Is makin' iron-poles,
And the mate upon the main hatch
Is cursin' all our souls.

For songs descriptive of whaling, in fact, a tabloid account of the entire cruise, there are few which can compare with the following, which has echoed in many a greasy forecastle of the old square-riggers.

Come, all ye bold seamen who are cruising for sperm.

Come, all ye jolly, bold seamen that have rounded Cape Horn.

For our captain has told us, and we hope he says true,

That there's plenty of sperm whales on the coast of Peru.

The first whale that we raised, it was late in the day,

Which caused our bold captain these kind words to say,

"Get ye down to your hammocks and there quietly lay.

We'll raise him in the morning at the break of the day."

'Twas early next morning, just as the sun rose,

That a man at the masthead sung out, "There she blows!"

"Where away?" cries the skipper, and the answer, from aloft,

"Three points on the lee bow and about two miles off."

"Then call up all hands and be of good cheer,

Get your lines in your boats and your tackle-falls clear.

Hoist and swing fore and aft, stand by each boat's crew.

Lower away, lower away, when the mainyard swings to."

Now the captain is fast and the whale has gone down,

And the chief mate lies waiting his line to bend on.

Now the whale has come up, like a log he did lay.

It can never be said that he gave us fair play.

And when the whale was safely alongside and the great, dripping, blanket-piece – every pound of which represented so much gold – was being cut in, the sweating, oil-soaked, greasy crew would burst into some such song as:

115

My father's a hedger and ditcher,
My mother does nothing but spin,
While I hunt whales for a living –
Good Lord, how the money comes in!

Like all "men who go down to the sea in ships," the whalemen were often sentimental and loved to moralize on their life and what it had in store and despite their vicious habits, their rough ways and the debasing, brutalizing life they led they were capable of real kindness, great sympathy and a keen appreciation of the beautiful. Although not sailors born, nor even accustomed to a seaman's life from early youth like the merchant sailors, yet the spell of the sea, the mystery of the trackless oceans, the marvels of the deep, the surpassing beauties of tropic islands or the majesty of stupendous icebergs and the vast silence and loneliness of night watches, all had their effect upon the men.

While many of them were of a class to which nothing but license and debauchery appealed, many more were men of intelligence, of good breeding and excellent antecedents, who had gone astray, while still others were scarcely more than boys, susceptible to any influence, and who had never known a kind word or a decent home and had run away to sea to escape what they imagined was a harder life ashore. Still others were men who had sought the forecastle of a whaleship for love of adventure, and a wish to "see the world," or had been lured by the exaggerated tales of fortunes to be made and the lurid advertisements of shipping agents; and one and all were heartily sick of whaling and terribly homesick before the cruise was over.

To some only obscene or profane songs were intelligible; to others songs of home appealed most strongly, while still others delighted in songs expressing sentiments which no one would have believed them capable of understanding. Time and time again, as the ship lazily rose and fell to the long swell of a mid-ocean calm, with canvas slapping the mast and rattling tackle-blocks as the trucks swept in wide arcs across the starlit sky, the crew would gather forward with pipes aglow, a battered accordion would be brought out and to the accompaniment of its wheezy notes some deep-throated whaleman would send his voice booming into the velvety blackness of the tropic night as he sung:

'Twas a love of adventure and a longing for gold,
And a hardened desire to roam
Tempted me far away o'er the watery world,
Far away from my kindred and home.
With a storm-beaten captain, so fearless and bold,
And a score of brave fellows or two,
Far away to the hardships, the hunger and cold,
Sailed this fearless and jovial crew.

Have you ever cruised on Diego's bold shores,
That are washed by the Antarctic wave,
Where the white-plumed albatross merrily soars
O'er many a poor whaler's grave?

Did you ever hear tell of that mighty sperm whale,
That when boldly attacked in his lair,
With one sweep of his mighty and ponderous tail
Sends the whaleboat so high in the air?

Did you ever join in with those heart-ringing cheers,
With your face turned to Heaven's blue dome
As laden with riches you purchased so dear
You hoisted your topsails, – bound home?

Up and down the seven seas the whalemen plied their trade, sung their songs and roared their chanteys. In the broiling doldrums, when the grease of years oozed from

117

the sun-scorched decks, their songs rang far across the brassy, waveless sea. Through dreary arctic nights, while the Aurora blazed like a curtain of rainbow-colored fire in the frosty heavens, the whalemen's songs echoed from precipitous glaciers and bergs and off wave-lashed shores of far Antarctic lands their songs startled the waddling penguins and roused sea-elephants from slumber.

And when at last the reeking hold could contain no more; when the weather-beaten ship was "fully laden" and the boats had been lowered for the last whale; then, as yards were squared for home, as the glad men hauled on the braces and the patched sails swelled to a fair wind and green seas rushed past lee rails in a smother of foam; then, these veterans of many a hard-fought battle worked with light hearts, for the cruise was over, hardships and privations would soon be but a memory of the past, ere long the twinkling lights of New Bedford would gleam beyond their bowsprit and with right good will the crew bellowed out this most joyful of all sea-songs:

We're homeward bound, oh, happy sound!
Goodbye, fare ye well,
Goodbye, fare ye well!
Come, rally the crew and run quick around,
Hurrah, my bullies, we're homeward bound!
Our yards we'll swing and our sails we'll set,
Good-bye, fare ye well,
Good-bye, fare ye well:
The whales we are leaving, we leave with regret,
Hurrah, my bullies, we're homeward bound!

Oh, heave with a will and heave long and strong,
Goodbye, fare ye well,
Goodbye, fare ye well!
Oh, sing a good chorus, for 'tis a good song,
Hurrah, my bullies, we're homeward bound!

We're homeward bound at last, they say,
Good-bye, fare ye well,
Good-bye, fare ye well!
Then tail on the braces and run her away:
Hurrah, my bullies, we're homeward bound!

We're homeward bound, may the winds blow fair;
Good-bye, fare ye well,
Good-bye, fare ye well!
Wafting us true to the friends waiting there,
Hurrah, my bullies, we're homeward bound!

MANY PERSONS ARE UNDER the impression that the decline in the whaling industry is due to the scarcity of whales – that the sea has been "fished out" of whales, so to speak, and that whales are practically exterminated. As a matter of fact, the very contrary is the case and whales are today more numerous, and are found nearer the whalemen's home ports than in the days when whaling was at its zenith. To be sure very large whales are not common – it takes a hundred years or more for a whale to attain full size – but medium-sized whales are so numerous as to more than make up for the lack of such giants as were once captured.

In this connection it is interesting to learn the actual size attained by whales and while records of whaling voyages deal more with the number of barrels obtained from whales than with measurements in feet, yet there are a number of cases where the sizes of whales were recorded in logbooks and by comparing the amount of oil obtained from these with other records, it is possible to obtain a very accurate idea of the largest whales ever taken.

There are numerous instances of 100-barrel or even 110-barrel whales, while 70- to 80-barrel whales were of everyday occurrence. The largest sperm whale of which I can find any record, in the way of measurements, was 90 feet long with flukes 18 feet across and a lower jaw 18 feet in length; this whale yielded over 100 barrels of oil. Another log records a sperm whale 79 feet in length with a breadth of flukes of 16 feet 6 inches, a length of jaw of 16 feet, and with a yield of 107 barrels of oil. As in these two cases both the dimensions in feet and the yield is given it is safe to assume that a whale which is 80 feet or more in length will give 100 barrels or more of oil and that the width of flukes and the length of lower jaws in adult sperm whales is practically one-fifth the entire length of the whale.

A short time ago Mr. Frank Wood of the Old Dartmouth Historical Society museum was offered the jaw of a sperm whale which measured 22 feet in length, and would indicate a whale measuring 110 feet in length – certainly a stupendous creature. That sperm whales as large or even larger than this have been taken is unquestionable, for in the New Bedford museum there are two teeth of such enormous size that by comparison the teeth from 80-foot whales appear like mere pigmies and judging from their size the sperm whale which owned them must have been fully 115 feet in length. Many jaws over 16 feet in length are preserved by whalers' families in the old New England ports, while logbooks are full of instances where 75 to 80-barrel whales were taken and 100 or even 110-barrel whales are frequently noted. All of which goes to prove that in the old whaling days sperm whales of from 75 to 100 feet in length were not unusual. Today, on the other hand, 60-foot sperm whales are rare, and few are taken which yield over 65 barrels, while 30, 20 or even 10-barrel whales are often killed – creatures scarcely larger than a good-sized grampus.

But the real secret of the decline of the New England whaling industry is not the scarcity or size of the whales, but the drop in the price of oil, the excessive increase in the cost of fitting out and operating ships, and the fact that steam whalers, darting-guns and extensive shore try-works, or boiling plants, have practically forced Yankee whalemen from the seas.

These remarks apply principally to sperm whaling, however, for Scotch whalers still hunt bowheads in the Arctic with profit and the steam-whaling vessels of Japan, Scandinavia and our own northwest coast hunt finbacks, gray whales, sulfur-bottoms and humpbacks and carry on a large and important industry.

Formerly sperm oil was the most valuable of all whale oil, and as sperm whales were found in almost all temperate and tropical seas they were more extensively hunted than any others of the whale tribe and the majority of the old-time whalemen were sperm whalers. Many of them, to be sure, caught right whales and bowheads and there were numerous ships which invariably went right whaling, but a glance at the records will show that the sperm oil brought in exceeded all other whale products in value.

Figures are always dry and tiresome, but only by means of a few figures can we obtain an idea of the decline of the whaling industry and the causes which brought it about. Up to December 1823, the largest cargo obtained on a three-years' voyage was 2,600 barrels valued at $65,000 and which was obtained by Captain Richmond of New Bedford. Thirty-four years before this William Swain of the ship *Ranger* returned with 1,000 barrels and stated that "no ship would ever take so much again" and in 1819 the captain of the *Independence* averred that no ship would ever again fill with oil.

But despite these predictions and their refutation by Captain Richmond, the ship *Sarah* of Nantucket came into port in 1830 with 3,497 barrels, worth over $89,000 – the largest cargo of oil ever brought to Nantucket from one voyage. By 1850 whaling had reached its topmost pinnacle and oil was worth over one dollar a gallon and the *Coral* returned from a three-years' voyage with 3,350 barrels, worth $126,630. Now let us glance at the results of cruises of recent years and we will find a paradoxical condition of affairs which casts to the winds the idea of whales being scarce, for in 1911 the brig *Sullivan*, during a cruise lasting but eleven weeks, obtained 1,500 barrels of sperm oil. Again, in the present year, 1915, the *Cameo* of New Bedford returned from a three-year cruise with 4,000 barrels, or over 600 barrels more than were ever before brought into port from a single cruise, even in the most prosperous days of the industry.

Notwithstanding this fact there is little profit in whaling today, for the Cameo's cargo is worth only $50,000 or about $15,000 less than the 2,600-barrel catch of Captain Richmond back in 1823 and less than one-half the value of the *Coral*'s catch in 1850. In other words, all other things being equal, a whaleman today must make a catch of something like 10,000 barrels to equal the gross receipts of a successful whaling cruise in 1850. To obtain such a cargo in three years is out of all question and aside from this, even if such a stupendous catch was made, the whaleman's profits would still be pitifully small compared to those of his predecessors of fifty or sixty years ago.

Besides the decrease in the price of sperm oil, which has dropped from one dollar, or even two dollars a gallon, of the fifties to thirty-five or forty cents a gallon today, there is the increased cost of fitting out to be considered.

Practically every article and item used on a whaleship has doubled or trebled in value within the past fifty years and some idea of how this affects the whaling industry may be gathered from the fact that the average cost of fitting a whaler for a two-years' cruise in 1790 was $12,000; in 1858 it had risen to $65,000, and today it has soared to the neighborhood of $150,000. Just one small item, but one of the most important to the whalemen, may be cited in this connection. The whaleboats, which in the heyday of whaling could be purchased for $80 each, today cost over $125.

To such causes as this the whaling industry of New England owes its decline; petroleum, stearine,[26] paraffin, gas, electricity and many other inventions or discoveries have contributed to the drop in the price of oil and gradually, but surely, the whaling industry has fallen off since it reached its greatest height in 1850.

In that year 736 vessels were devoted to whaling and hailed from a dozen or more New England ports, and from

---

[26] White crystalline substance of fatty acids used in candle making.

their voyages they returned with 14,744 barrels of sperm oil, 39,215 barrels of whale oil, and 894,700 pounds of whalebone.

In 1851 New Bedford and its neighbor, Fairhaven, could boast of 314 vessels employing an army of nearly 10,000 men which brought in 10,636 barrels of sperm oil, 86,451 barrels of whale oil, and 602,100 pounds of whalebone in one season.

Then commenced the decline and by 1877 the entire whaling fleet had dropped to less than 200 ships. By 1881 only 171 whaling vessels flew the Stars and Stripes and 123 of these claimed New Bedford as their home port. In 1880, 37,614 barrels of sperm oil; 34,626 barrels of whale oil and 458,400 pounds of whalebone was the catch of this pitifully small fleet, while today – only thirty-four years later – the total catch of sperm oil brought to New Bedford in 1915 was but 10,000 barrels while not a pound of bone nor a barrel of right whale oil has entered New Bedford's harbor for several years.

Like many another industry, whaling has always had its ups and downs, its years of tremendous success and great prosperity and its years of misfortune, losses and dejection. Few industries, however, have risen to such heights and fallen to such depths as whaling, and over and over again the New England whalemen have been practically driven from the seas, only to reappear in greater numbers and with greater strength, determination and success.

The first real setback which the whalers received occurred in 1741, when French and Spanish privateers penetrated Davis Straits, and even entered Vineyard Sound, where they captured and destroyed whaling vessels of the English colonists. Despite the risks incurred the courageous Nantucket whalemen continued to ply their trade, but so many of their vessels were taken by the enemy that by 1750 the Davis Straits were abandoned as too dangerous.

With the ceding of Canada to Great Britain,[27] the Gulf of St. Lawrence and the Straits of Belle Isle were opened to the whalemen, and by 1761 many Nantucket vessels were capturing whales in these waters and the industry was again resuming its importance to southern New England, for even in those early days whaling had become of vast importance and in 1774 over 360 vessels and 4,700 men were devoted exclusively to whaling.

Scarcely had the whalemen recovered from the raids of the French when the Revolutionary War broke out and the lanterns that glowed from the spire of Old North Church and sent Paul Revere upon his famous ride, foretold the death of countless whalemen, the loss of hundreds of ships, and the knell of the whaling industry for many years to come.

Before the war America had 360 whaling vessels and England less than 100, and when at last peace was declared and the United States became independent, the whaling vessels flying the Stars and Stripes totaled but 80 while those flying the banner of England numbered 314.

But still greater than the loss of ships was the toll of death among the brave American whalemen. Ships could be built, boats could be equipped and money could be obtained, but the men themselves could not be replaced. No place suffered more from the depredations of the British than Nantucket, for of the 150 ships destroyed by the English 134 hailed from this little island and in the 800 families in Nantucket there were 202 widows and 342 orphans, while 1,200 men had been killed or captured by the enemy and the monetary loss amounted to ten million dollars.

Scarcely had peace been declared when with the indomitable spirit which always characterized the whaleman, new ships were built, whalers again set forth, and by 1791 six ships had sailed for the Pacific from

---

[27] France officially ceded Canada to Great Britain in 1763, through the Treaty of Paris.

Nantucket, accompanied by one vessel from New Bedford. Even before this, however, the whalemen had been cruising in nearer waters and one vessel, which sailed from Sag Harbor in 1785, returned to New Bedford in 1787 with a full cargo, while the brig *Bedford* of Nantucket, American-built and American-manned, had loaded with 487 butts of oil and sailed for England, the first ship to fly the American flag in a British port. By 1790 the whaling industry was again at full tide, whales were abundant, and vessels came in from short cruises with tremendous catches – some with over 1,000 barrels – and the British became alarmed for fear the entire fishery would fall into the hands of the Americans.

Finding her own whalemen apathetic and unable to compete with the Yankees, England used every endeavor to induce the New England whalemen to settle in British territory and a number emigrated to Europe and Canada.

Once more war threatened and during 1798 the Americans lost many of their ships to the French. Although this resulted in untold hardships and misery for the whalemen's families, and many who were formerly well-to-do died in poverty, yet the claims have never been settled, the losses to those who gave their all to aid in building our prosperity have never been repaid, and the whole matter forms one of the most disgraceful pages and darkest blots in the history of our country. Fortunately for the whalemen the trouble with France was of short duration and at its close the whaling fleet rapidly increased until the War of 1812 broke out. The beginning of the war found Yankee whaleships scattered far and wide upon the oceans, and though many hurried for the protection of New York, Boston and other fortified towns great numbers were seized and destroyed by British privateers and men-o'-war.

This was particularly the case in the Pacific and matters were made still worse by the action of the Peruvian Government which declared itself an ally of England. Vessels in Peruvian ports were seized, the men were imprisoned, and finally the Honorable Joel R. Poinsett of South Carolina was dispatched to Peru to adjust matters.

Upon his arrival he found the country in a state of chaos and diplomatic efforts proving unavailing, he promptly joined the army of one faction, and with a force of 400 men and 3 guns defeated 1,500 men with 2 men-o'-war and released the vessels and imprisoned whalemen at Talcahuano. Soon after this, Captain Porter with his fleet was sent to the Pacific, where he captured and destroyed the British ships, turned the tables on the English and insured safety to the Americans. But for long after there was hard feeling between our whalemen and the British, and wherever Yankees and English met hard words, harder blows and cracked heads were the results. It was on one such occasion that an overbearing British officer challenged an American whaleman to a duel, whereupon the latter selected harpoons as weapons and the Englishman promptly apologized and withdrew.

The end of the War of 1812 found the New England whaling ports perfect beehives of activity and bustle, and by the first of January 1816, over 30 Yankee whaleships were cruising in the Pacific and Indian Oceans, from Nantucket alone, and by July the first ship returned from a six weeks' cruise with 100 barrels of oil.

New Bedford now came to the fore as a whaling port and her ships dotted the surface of the seven seas. The offshore grounds of the Pacific were discovered by the Globe of Nantucket in 1818, the ship Maro found the Japan grounds in 1819 and returned with 2,425 barrels of sperm oil, and by the next season thirty ships and more were hunting whales off the coast of Nippon.

So numerous were the ships and so tremendous the slaughter that the whalemen were constantly compelled to search for new grounds, and thus the South Sea Islands were discovered, their unknown channels and uncharted reefs were traversed and the cannibal natives saw white men for the first time. To many of the men the beautiful tropic isles and the easy life appealed strongly and as some of the inhabitants were friendly not a few whalemen left their ships and joined the islanders. One deserter, David Whippey, of Nantucket, married a native woman of Fiji, became a prominent man and a sub-chief, and afterwards, in 1839, was appointed American vice-consul and proved a very capable and useful man.

So keen were the whalemen to find new grounds that Zanzibar was visited, the distant Seychelles were reached and one captain even entered the Red Sea. From these far-distant and unknown lands the whalemen returned, laden with riches, and their strange tales of the countries, their accounts of the people and their narratives of the cannibal practices of the savages led to exploring expeditions and missionaries being sent out and ere long the reefs of the South Seas were surveyed and charted, trading vessels followed the whalers and Christianity was spread far and wide among the natives. Then commenced the Golden Age of the whaling industry, for right whales were discovered on the Kodiak grounds in 1835, the first bowhead was taken in the North Pacific off the coast of Kamchatka by the Janus of New Bedford in 1843, and the bark *Superior* took the first whale in the Arctic after passing Bering Strait in 1844. Thus the Arctic soon became a famous ground and by 1846 the American whaling fleet consisted of 678 ships and barks, 35 brigs and 44 schooners valued at over twenty-one million dollars.

With this great increase in the number of vessels, the enormous catches made, and the unparalleled profits, the cost of ships and outfitting increased, the price of oil fell from over-production, and many vessels dropped out and many ports gave up the whaling business. But other ports soon filled the gaps and when, in 1850, the whaling industry reached its zenith, there were 736 vessels under the American flag and of these over 300 hailed from New Bedford.

Then came the Civil War, with the great fleet of whaleships scattered far and wide on three- and four-year cruises, and when at the close of hostilities the last ship was accounted for the fleet had been reduced to 163 vessels.

To the cruisers and privateers of the Confederates many of the whalers fell easy victims, while many others were decoyed and destroyed by treachery. When a vessel was captured the Confederates would wait until nightfall, and then setting fire to their prize, would lie in wait to seize and destroy the unsuspecting whalemen who hurried to rescue companions whom they thought were in peril by fire.

The result of the raids of the Confederates was soon apparent, for the whalemen who escaped sold their ships to be used as merchantmen, laid them up until the war should end or placed them under the neutral flag of Hawaii.

In addition some forty of the whaleships were purchased by the government and formed the larger part of the famous "Stone Fleet," which, in 1861, was sunk off Charlestown and Savannah to prevent the entrance or exit of blockade runners and privateers.

Many of the men thus thrown out of employment, and no doubt only too glad to avenge their injuries upon their enemies, enlisted in the Northern navy, and of the 5,986 naval officers who served the Union, Massachusetts furnished 1,226, Maine 449, Connecticut 264 and Rhode Island 102 – many of them former whalemen, whose training as sailors, whose lives of daring and danger, and whose unequaled courage and self-reliance well fitted them to become sea-fighters. Despite the havoc wrought by the Confederates and the superior speed and armament of their vessels they did not always find the whalers easy victims, and many whalemen showed wonderful bravery and heroism when attacked by their enemies. Among these was Captain Thomas G. Young of the Fairhaven bark[28] *Favorite.*

In 1865 the *Shenandoah* was cruising in the North Pacific when, after capturing and sinking five ships in Behring Strait, she discovered a fleet of whalers helping salvage the *Brunswick* of New Bedford which had been caught in the ice and destroyed. Among these vessels was the Favorite, and as the Shenandoah was seen approaching Captain Young loaded all his firearms, darting-guns and bomb-lances and took his stand on the cabin roof. As the boat from the *Shenandoah* came alongside the brave whaleman ordered the Confederates to keep off, and the officer, reading death and determination in the Yankee's grim face, wisely withdrew and returned to his ship. The Shenandoah then trained a gun on the *Favorite*, the gunner was ordered to fire low and a shot crashed through the bark. Even then Captain Young remained defiant and to the remonstrances of his officers, at the useless risk he was taking, he replied that he would die happy if he could but shoot Waddell, the commander of the *Shenandoah.*

Finding arguments useless, and believing the captain had gone mad, the mates managed surreptitiously to remove the ammunition and caps from the arms and then took to the boats, leaving the gallant skipper alone upon his ship. Captain Waddell then sent a boat's crew to secure the whaleman and the officer in charge boarded the bark to haul down her flag. No sooner did the Confederate step upon the deck than the skipper leveled a musket and pulled trigger and then, finding his weapons useless, he resisted the other with his fists. Drawing his pistol the Confederate threatened to shoot, whereupon the Yankee captain replied, "Shoot and be damned," but at this moment the armed boat's crew reached the deck, the captain was overpowered and finding further resistance use-less he surrendered. One would think that such a brave and

---

[28] Also spelled barque, a bark is a term for any sailing ship boasting three or more masts.

heroic defense of his property would have won admiration and respect from his captors, but to the everlasting shame of Captain Waddell the gallant whaleman was placed in irons, robbed of all his personal possessions and was treated like a common malefactor.

Sometimes too, the whaleships were put to most unexpected uses and the weather-beaten, unromantic skippers became veritable knight errants, albeit they were impelled to their Quixotic deeds by love of promised reward rather than by disinterested motives. Such was the voyage of the *Catalpa*, a New Bedford whaleship which set forth from the little Massachusetts town ostensibly on a whaling cruise, but in reality for a very different purpose.

Although the *Catalpa* actually went a-whaling and took oil, yet her ultimate destination was Fremantle, Australia, and the real object of her voyage to liberate and carry away the Fenian prisoners confined there. In her mission the *Catalpa* was successful, but in accomplishing it her company met with adventures and experiences which make a most thrilling and romantic tale.

The prime mover and organizer of the expedition was John W. Goff, later Justice of the Supreme Court, and prominent among those who took part in the project, in fact the actual leader, was Mr. Thomas Brennan, who, until his death in New York in November 1915, was the last survivor of the expedition.

On April 29, 1875, the *Catalpa*, Captain Anthony, cleared from New Bedford and a year later returned to New York with the six rescued Fenians who had been sentenced to life imprisonment in Australia. Mr. Brennan's mission was to join the expedition at the Azores. He went there on board the *Gazelle* with a case of firearms and a large sum of money to defray many incidental expenses. The *Catalpa*, however, had cleared from the islands, and Mr. Brennan was instructed to go to England.

Passage on board the *Selbourne*, the only vessel which was leaving for England, was refused to him. So Mr.

Brennan and several others concealed themselves on board. They were made prisoners later by the master of the ship, who professed to believe them to be criminals endeavoring to escape from justice. Mr. Brennan's predicament was serious, especially as he had been a political fugitive from England several years before, following the uprising of 1865.[29] Nothing daunted, he left the ship when near Liverpool, and was picked up by the crew of a small boat, when nearly drowned. He reached London without further adventure and after consulting friends, started for Australia, where Captain Anthony, of the *Catalpa*, meanwhile awaited reinforcements. After a series of mishaps, he, with remarkable fortitude, reached a secluded part of the coast and finally put out on board the *Catalpa*, at a place known as Rotten Nest, twenty-eight miles from Fremantle.

The story of the march twenty-eight miles through the bush to the prison, the daring rescue and the return march is one of the most exciting ever recounted. Countless hardships were endured by rescuers and rescued alike, and when all were finally on board the *Catalpa* and the whaler was under way they were pursued at sea by a ship pressed into service by the British authorities and manned by infantry and artillery. The ship was the *Georgette*. When the commander of the troops on board ordered the master of the *Catalpa* to heave to and surrender the prisoners, Captain Anthony coolly pointed to the Stars and Stripes at the staff and told the English officer to "fire away."

But the British declined to accept this invitation and the *Catalpa* sailed safely away, bearing the rescued men to the United States and freedom.

It would be pleasant indeed to think that every American whaleman was as gallant and patriotic as Captain

---

[29] The Morant Bay rebellion was an unsuccessful attempted coup of British colony Jamaica.

Young, or that every Yankee whaleship was put to such romantic purposes as the *Catalpa* when not cruising for whales, but unfortunately such is not the case. Many of the whalemen were as black-hearted, soulless villains as ever lived and were willing to commit any crime or take any risk if promised rich returns. Finding whaling less profitable than in former years with ships and reckless crews of rascals under their command, not a few of the Yankee whalemen, who set sail ostensibly for whales, converted their vessels into slavers and trafficked in human beings.

With slavery abolished by Great Britain[30] and the slave trade suppressed by force of arms the price of negroes reached undreamed-of figures in many of the South American countries and the West Indies. To men as reckless, as daring, and as utterly heartless and unprincipled as were many of the whalers this opportunity to reap enormous profits was too attractive to resist. Picking up cargoes of slaves on the coast of Africa the whaleships set sail for the Caribbean, their dark, unventilated, stinking holes crowded with men, women and children whose sufferings were unspeakable.

Day after day the bodies of those who perished were cast to the waiting sharks, as the ships sailed slowly westward, or laid becalmed beneath the blazing tropical sun. But the whalers could well afford to lose a portion of their human freight – the profits from those who survived would be ample – and they cared no more for the tortures, the agonies and the sufferings of the blacks than for the dying flurry of a stricken whale.

If no warships' sails were sighted and all went well, the fate of the slaves was frightful enough, but if a suspicious sail lifted itself above the rim of the sea and the whalemen recognized the stranger as a man-o'-war, the doom of the

[30] Britian abolished slavery in 1807, however the slave trade in its overseas colonies (the British Empire) continued until 1838.

slaves was sealed, for with the utmost dispatch they were driven on deck, chained together, weighted with shot and cast living into the sea – to sink forever and destroy all evidence of the ships' true calling.

And this dark chapter of whaling was not of the long distant past – scarcely fifty years ago many a Puritanical, New England family received its income from this diabolical trade and in old New Bedford papers one may find ample proofs.

Fortunately a number of the whalemen slavers were captured and met with their just deserts and in the New Bedford Shipping List of December 3, 1861, the following item appears:

In the U. S. Court in Boston on Friday, Judge Clifford sentenced Samuel P. Skinner, convicted of fitting out the barque *Margaret Scott* of New Bedford for the slave trade, to pay a fine of $1,000 and to be confined at hard labor for the term of five years in the jail at Taunton.

In the same year the bark *Brutus* of New Bedford fitted out for a slave voyage and succeeded in landing a cargo of 650 blacks in Cuba, but one of her owners was convicted and served several years in the penitentiary while others were heavily fined. Every effort was made to suppress the trade, numerous convictions were made, and gradually the business was abandoned, while the ships, seized and condemned by the authorities, were loaded with stone, sent south, and were sunk to block the harbors of the Confederate ports.

10 - THE PASSING OF THE WHALER

FOR HALF A CENTURY the fate of Yankee whalemen has been sealed, but they have died hard and, as their ancestors battled with the elements and with maddened whales, the last of the whalemen have waged a courageous if futile struggle against the overwhelming odds of fate, modem progress and twentieth-century civilization.

A few weather-beaten ancient hookers still sail forth from old New Bedford's harbor, but no longer do the shippers advertise for "five hundred brave Americans" as of yore, for scarce that number of Americans could be found today among the crews of all the whaling vessels that bear the name "New Bedford" upon their counters, and the old-time Yankee skipper is no more.

New Bedford, once the greatest whaling port in all the world, whose name was known on all the seven seas and in the uttermost parts of the globe, is now a busy manufacturing town. Looms and spindles have taken the place of whaleboat and harpoon and within a short time the whaling industry will be but a memory of the past.

Today the famous old barks and ships lie moored, forsaken, at the wharves, a few grizzled old whaling captains still survive to tell of past experiences, docks still may be seen covered with casks of oil and vessels still set forth on long cruises to return, oil-laden, to the Massachusetts port; but they are not Yankee whaleships, but small schooners belonging to an alien race.

No longer is there a fortune in whaling; no more do thousands of artisans and laborers depend upon the whaling industry for their livelihood; no longer does a steady stream of gold flow into New Bedford from the oil and bone so bravely won. A few still make a living from whaling, but the romance, adventure and mystery of the whaleman's calling have gone forever and never again will he sing as of yore:

'Twas a love of adventure, a longing for gold,
And a hardened desire to roam,
Tempted me far away o'er the watery world,
Far away from my kindred and home.

Neither gold nor adventure comes much into the life of the whaleman of today and his roaming seldom carries him beyond the Azores or the Antilles, for the whaling industry of New England has gone into the hands of the Portuguese and their schooners cruise the Atlantic on prosaic, matter-of-fact business lines.

No one seems to know just when the Portuguese whalemen superseded the Americans, but today scarcely any others can be found and even the officers and captains are Portuguese from the Western Islands. For many years – one might almost say for centuries – whaling vessels have touched at Cape de Verde or the Azores and have added a few Portuguese to their crews. They are good whalemen, hard workers, quiet, law-abiding and obedient, and gradually their numbers have increased and the whaling business has become theirs.

But even to the Portuguese the whaleships today offer few inducements; they can earn far better wages working as laborers ashore, and while it's easy enough to pick up a crew on the homeward trip – for the Portuguese are glad to work their passage to the States – when the ship is ready to sail out it is a different story. There are few better businessmen than the Portuguese, few who realize better than they how little profit may be expected in whaling today, and as long as they can find employment ashore they have no desire to become whalemen. Only by the utmost economy, the strictest attention to details, and the best of good luck, can the Portuguese make a living from whaling; and though whales are more abundant than ever, though marvelous catches are made, and though the Portuguese can live and keep up their vessels very cheaply, yet even they are gradually abandoning the industry.

By transferring their catch to a vessel sent to Dominica they can remain on the grounds for several seasons. By using small schooners – which are often condemned and cannot be insured – they reduce the cost of whaling to a minimum, and as their catches are often remarkable a few of the Portuguese captains do very well indeed. But in other parts of the world whaling still is carried on, and on an enormous scale, and is a most important industry. The huge, steam Scotch whalers still cruise among the icefloes of the Arctic and find it profitable, and in Scandinavia, Japan, and on our own northwestern coasts whaling has been systematized and developed into a most important and lucrative business.

By means of powerful steamers equipped with the latest types of swivel-guns, darting guns, and bomb-lances, the great finbacks and sulfur-bottoms are killed. The carcasses are inflated with compressed air to prevent them from sinking and are then towed to the rendering plant. Here they are hauled up skidways by steam, they are stripped of blubber, the oil is tried out, and the flesh, bones and other material is converted into fertilizer.

This is not real whaling, however – there is not the slightest element of danger, romance or adventure in it and many an old Yankee whaleman would rise in his grave to protest if such methods were mentioned in the same breath as his own brave and adventurous deeds.

Fifty years ago a dozen New England ports owed their very existence to whaling; a score of years past a forest of masts, a maze of rigging and a labyrinth of yards crossed and recrossed the skyline of New Bedford's waterfront and that of many another port. A decade later many a bluff-bowed bark and ship reared her dingy sides above New Bedford's docks and one could scarce glance harbor-wise without seeing the masts and yards of a whaleship at the end of a street. Even in 1914 a dozen and more square-riggers were moored at New Bedford's wharves at one time.

Today, one may travel the length and breadth of New Bedford's waterfront without seeing a crossed yard and one may search in vain in New London, Nantucket, Sag Harbor, Provincetown, Bristol or Falmouth for a whaleship. By the sides of Merrill's Wharf one may find a few ramshackle, prosaic schooners whose vocation is evident by the greasy decks, the lookout's hoops at the mastheads and the oil casks lying near at hand, and in out-of-the-way slips at Fairhaven one may still find a few picturesque, old, square-rigged vessels, dismantled, weather-beaten and abandoned.

There is something sad and pitiful about these sturdy old ships now out of commission. Through years and years they plowed the wide oceans of the globe; they crunched amid the ice-floes of the Arctic; Antarctic gales howled through their frayed and rotten rigging and their masts and yards bleached under the rays of tropic suns. Above their trucks have loomed the desolate mountains of Kerguelen and the castellated pinnacles of mighty icebergs. About them have gathered fur-clad Eskimos in kayaks of skin and around them have swarmed swift proas[31] loaded with laughing, copper-skinned beauties of the South Seas. Through their broad gangways have been hoisted untold tons of reeking blubber and their upper masts are black as ebony from the smoke of countless boilings. Within their kennel-like forecastles have echoed the sea-songs of generations of hairy-chested whalemen and on many of their decks has been spilled the life-blood of human beings.

What stories they could tell if they could but speak! What tales of marvelous adventures, of grim tragedy and human sufferings, what narratives of license, debauchery and unbridled passion! But the wonderful scenes their

---

[31] General term for a multi-hull outrigger sailboat popular in the Southern Hemisphere.

lofty masts have looked upon, the terrific tempests their broad bows have breasted and the marvels of strange waters in which their anchors have been dropped, will never be known. They are but mute testimonials of whaling's Golden Age, relics that link the present with the past and soon even they will be gone, broken up for junk and torn to pieces for the metal and the rigging – surely an ignominious ending for such gallant craft. One cannot help wishing that they might find a better fate – given to the "god of winds, the lightning and the gale" which they have so long defied.

Never again will such ships be built – they are of the dead and gone past – but they deserve a place in our history, a niche in our national museums, and a warm spot in our hearts, for in them the stoutest-hearted of all mariners sailed up and down the world. From their mastheads Old Glory fluttered as bravely in arctic gales as in tropic trade wind; their keels traced the tracks into which flowed the commerce, civilization and Christianity of the world and they played as important a part in making our country what it is as did the Liberty Bell, Old North Church or any other hallowed relic of our early days.

And if this can be said of the battered hulks that still lie, unhonored and unsung, awaiting the junk man and dissolution, what can be said of the men who sailed in them?

We honor the names of our pioneers on land – Crockett, Boone, Lewis, Clarke, Bowie and a score of others are familiar names to every schoolboy – but how many know even the least about the whalemen? Pioneers of civilization, leaders in exploration, founders of commerce, forerunners of the Christian faith, they knew not fear and laughed at death. The five oceans and the seven seas were their hunting grounds, the frozen wastes of polar regions or the torrid tropics were equally their haunt, but their hearts remained always true to the green New England hills and the granite-ribbed coasts of the land they loved so well.

But if the world at large has forgotten the part they played in building our nation, old New Bedford has borne them well in mind, has recognized their valor and their worth, and has erected a splendid monument in honor of her whaling sons.

From a monolith of Massachusetts granite protrudes the bronze replica of a whaleboat. In the bow, with wind-tossed hair and poised iron, stands the heroic figure of a whaleman and deeply graven in the stone is the motto: "A dead whale or a stove boat."

It is the very epitome of the spirit of the whalemen of the past and a fitting tribute to the "whalemen whose skill, hardihood and daring brought fame and fortune to New Bedford and made its name known in every seaport of the globe," as inscribed upon this magnificent monument.

Deeply indeed is it to be regretted that progress has robbed us of the picturesque figures, the glorious deeds, and the deep-sea romance of our whalers of the past; that steam and, modern guns have replaced the stately, white-winged ships and home-wrought weapons – even though they may live on as cherished memories.

Erelong, the last old-school Yankee whaleman will have passed into the great beyond and as he sights the harbor lights of that port from which none return, his mind will turn to days long gone and with his last breath he will murmur the final stanza of the whalers' song:

Did you ever join in with heart-ringing cheers,
And your face turned to Heaven's blue dome,
As laden with riches you purchased so dear,
You hoisted your topsails, bound home?

Made in the USA
Middletown, DE
02 May 2024

53782070R00080